Understanding the Ancient
Secrets of the Horse's Mind

Robert M. Miller, D.V.M.

The Russell Meerdink Co., Ltd.
1555 South Park Avenue
Neenah, WI 54956 USA
(920) 725-0955 Worldwide
Printed in the United States of America

Library of Congress - Cataloging-in-Publication Data

Miller, Robert M.
    Understanding the ancient secrets of the horse's mind / Robert M.
Miller.
        p. cm.
    Includes bibliographical references (p.) and index.
    ISBN 0-929346-65-3
        1.   Horses--Behavior. 2. Horses--Training. I. Title.

SF281 .M565 1999
636.1'0835--dc21   99-046591

                                                              CIP

Associate Editor: Cynthia Halas Dery

Published by:

The Russell Meerdink Company, Ltd.
1555 South Park Avenue
Neenah, WI 54956 USA
(920) 725-0955

Printed in the United States of America

Disclaimer

While the techniques and methods described in this book are drawn from the author's extensive experience and knowledge, this book is not all-inclusive on the subject matter and may not apply in all circumstances. This book is not intended to be a training manual. The reader should consult with and seek the advice of a professional trainer or competent horseperson when considering applying these techniques on his or her particular horse or in a specific circumstance. Neither the author nor the publisher assume any liability or make any guarantees of any nature for any outcome resulting from the use of the procedures or techniques described herein.

Dedication

To those horsemen, past and present, who saw the light and forsook tradition to train horses with gentle, persuasive and non-forceful methods, and who took the trouble to publish their knowledge. Without their wisdom, I could never have learned in a single lifetime what I know about horses.

Acknowledgements

I have learned from all the horsemen I have encountered in my life. Sadly, what I learned from most of them was to avoid using their traditional coercive and sometimes brutal methods. However, from books - some of them very old - and from a few enlightened individuals, I learned that there are better ways. The list includes M. Horace Hayes, John Rarey, Ed Connell, D. Magner, Monte Foreman, John Richard Young, Dr. Jim McCall, Bill and Tom Dorrance, Tom Roberts, Maurice Wright, Monty Roberts, Pat Parelli, Richard Shrake, Ray Hunt, and Buck Brannaman. There were others, and people like them helped to make us a little more civilized, and made the world a better place for the long suffering horse.

I would like to acknowledge the *Journal of Equine Veterinary Science*, the official journal of the World Equine Veterinary Association. Much of the material in this book was first published as articles in this journal.

Table of Contents

8

Introduction

Horses are more effectively trained with persuasive methods rather than with coercive methods. This concept motivated me to write this book. Persuasive methods, that elicit behavior that the horse *wants* to do, are safer, faster and longer lasting than are coercive methods that elicit behavior that the horse *must* do.

Why then have coercive methods been the principle training techniques used by all human cultures?

It is because such methods are natural to us. We are a predatory, aggressive species and this is generally more true if we are young and male. The horse, by contrast, is a prey species. It is timid and easily frightened. Its response to fear is flight. Harnessed, controlled flight can be obtained by using physical force, pain and coercion. Jumping, racing, driving and even dressage movements are simply controlled flight responses that have become conditioned responses. But, horses run for joy and pleasure, not just from fear.

The horse, being a flight creature, as is abundantly and repeatedly emphasized in this book, experiences anxiety in response to certain emotions when they are displayed by a human handler. These emotions are anger and impatience.

Anger and impatience are incompatible with good horsemanship. Both intimidate the horse and stimulate the instinct to run away, or, if the horse thinks that it cannot flee, then these emotions may precipitate an alternative defense, such as kicking, striking, or biting.

It is only human to experience such emotions. The test of our character, however, is whether or not we are capable of suppressing these feelings, rise above them and allow civility and reason to cope with the situation. Therefore, in dealing with horses, if we allow reason to dictate our behavior, we will greatly enhance our ability to communicate with them and to understand their behavior.

Although coercion and force have been the primary means by which mankind has trained horses to serve his needs throughout history, far better means exist. These means are more humane, more civilized, more intelligent, more effective and actually easier to implement (once we learn to use them and to suppress our normal human predatory instincts). That's what this book is about.

Non-coercive training techniques produce equine athletes which perform well and enjoy doing it. This is achieved by means of the behavior shaping techniques described in this book and especially by control of movement. Of course, many traditional trainers will reject this concept. To the skeptics I point out that an older mare almost invariably leads wild horses. Indeed, she is often a decrepit older mare, certainly not the physically strongest individual in the herd. How is this possible? Shouldn't the leadership be accorded to the fleetest and strongest?

No! It is awarded to the wise, experienced, older individual and that position is maintained by *assertively controlling the movement of the other members of the herd.* We can do the same thing. This is the principle underlying the *Revolution in Horsemanship* or what is now being called "Natural Horsemanship." Why the latter designation? Because it is natural to the horse, not to the human.

The term "leadership" needs definition because I am using it as a synonym for dominance. Dominance is a word that immediately alienates many people. However, it is a scientifically correct word and rather than avoid its use in this book, I prefer to define it so readers will understand it.

"Dominance" means *leadership* and it is absolutely essential therefore, in order to lead a horse, we *dominate* it. Now many people, including some trainers I respect, will deny that fact, but it is nevertheless true. *All* good horse trainers get the results they do because their horses accept their leadership, whether the person is on the ground or on the horse's back. Some trainers, denying dominance, assert that they have developed a "partnership" with the horse and that it does not involve dominance. Nonsense! Such a trainer, however effective, simply does not understand the concept of dominance. As is explained repeatedly in this book, *dominance is established not by cruelty and aggressiveness, but by control of movement.* All good horse trainers do this and thereby dominate the horses they work with. Certainly a partnership exists, but the human must be the leader.

10

Actually there is nothing new about the kind of horsemanship we are talking about. A few talented trainers have always used it but now, for the first time, this non-confrontational, humane, swift and effective training philosophy is becoming popular worldwide. Why? Because today's horse owners are better educated, more receptive to the science of psychology and because of the information explosion that is occurring in most technologies. Videos, publications and jet travel allow clinicians to travel rapidly to spread the word. These people are advancing the art of horsemanship so quickly that most of the traditional methods of the past will soon become obsolete. It is also significant that, for the first time in human history, women dominate the horse industry. Women, as a rule, are very receptive to non-confrontational, resistance-free, gentler and kinder methods of training horses.

During my life I have worked with thousands of horses. A veterinarian's work is always frightening to horses, often uncomfortable and sometimes painful. Many of the horses I worked with were poorly trained, often unbroke, sometimes aggressive.

In spite of all this, I was only hospitalized once in all those years as a result of an injury caused by an equine patient. Before I went to veterinary school, I worked with a lot of horses as a farm and ranch hand, colt breaker and rodeo contestant. Many of these horses were downright dangerous, yet none of the injuries I incurred required hospitalization. It is significant that my own horses caused many of the injuries I suffered. Why? Because "familiarity breeds contempt." I learned defensive horsemanship techniques working around other peoples' dangerous or ill-behaved horses. Yet, around my own trusted horses I sometimes let my guard down and under those circumstances I was hurt.

I can personally attest to how much horses can improve one's basic qualities. I am an impatient person. Horses taught me patience. I don't think I've ever been unkind, but having been a normal young male, horses sometimes provoked me to aggressiveness. They taught me, sometimes painfully, to be kinder and more tolerant. I have a fairly volatile personality being quick to laugh, to cry and to anger. Horses taught me to contain my emotions. They taught me the futility of losing my temper. They increased my awareness, my perceptivity and my compassion. Above all, they taught me that far more can be accomplished with persuasion than with coercion.

It is said so often that it has become trite, but it is true that, "the outside of a horse is good for the inside of a human being." We benefit by our contact with this unique and beautiful animal. My hope is that this can be accomplished without injury to either horse or human.

So, the best way to train horses is to do so using love and leadership and with that in mind, let's consider the secrets that science has uncovered which explain the horse's mind.

Robert M. Miller, D.V.M.
Thousand Oaks, California
November, 1999

Chapter 1

The Ten Ancient Secrets
Of the Horse's Mind

The history of the human race and that of the horse are closely intertwined. The human fascination with horses dates back to our caveman ancestors and, perhaps, even beyond that. The earliest recorded history of mankind is in the form of drawings etched into the stone walls of caves. Many of these drawings are depictions of horses. When archeologists uncover remains of ancient civilizations, more times than not, they also discover evidence that horses were part of the social and economic structure.

Many facets of the human fascination with horses are understandable. As horses became domesticated, they became beasts of burden. They were used to till fields, pull heavy loads and transport goods and passengers from place to place. Horses brought prosperity to those cultures that learned to domesticate them. Horses extended the range over which men could explore, hunt, trade and wage war. An army traveling and fighting on horseback has a distinct advantage over one that is on foot. The horse is also an important item of our social fabric. Competitions, races and games involving men and horses are as old as man's domestication of the animal itself.

Not all of our fascination with horses can be explained in practical or utilitarian terms. The grace and beauty of the horse enthralls us today in the same way it enthralled caveman artists of many millennia ago. Horses are living works of art. On any given day, more people pause along roadsides to enjoy the beauty of a horse galloping across the field than there are visitors to all the art museums in the world. And horses have always been subtle symbols of wealth and power. The Bedouin tribesmen of the Arabian desert are quick to point out that "a man's treasure is carried in the bellies of his mares." There are few in Kentucky who would disagree!

Above all else, it is probably the mystique of the horse that so fascinates and perplexes us humans. Embodied in the horse is the same range of abstract and intangible personality characteristics that we find in ourselves. Judged from the human perspective, some horses, like some people, are fearful and others bold; some have a strong work ethic and others are lazy; some appear to have the desire to win and while others are non-competitive; some react rationally to situations, others irrationally; some always seem to be good-natured while others are hostile; and, some are said to be honest and others dishonest. Perhaps our desire to understand the horse is nothing more than a desire to understand ourselves and the people around us.

For hundreds of years we have used selective breeding to influence what our horses will look like and how they will move. By careful mating, we can influence the horse's size, color and shape. We can breed horses that will run faster races, pull heavier loads, cut calves out of the herd more nimbly, or endure long treks through uninviting terrain. We can genetically influence whether a horse will prefer one gait over another, whether its neck will be long or short, its nose dished or level.

Despite all of this selective breeding, the foal born in your stable last night inherited the same ten traits, as did the horses depicted on the wall of the caveman. These ten, inherited traits influence how the horse perceives the world around it and how it reacts to its environment. These traits include anatomical, physiological and behavioral characteristics that are intimately linked. The ten traits determine how the horse responds to training and interacts with its handlers and other horses. These ten traits are embedded deep within its DNA and are shared, without exception, by every horse that was ever born. When one understands the ten traits, the personality of the horse is not as mysterious as it first appeared.

True horsepeople understand these ten traits and use them both as a means of influencing the horse to respond in a predictable fashion and as a means of avoiding the danger inherent in being around horses.

No horse can fulfill its potential unless its trainer understands the ten traits. No horseperson will ever fulfill his or her potential without first understanding the ten traits. No person is safe working around horses without first understanding the ten traits.

Here is a summary of the ten traits every horse inherits. The following chapters discuss each trait in detail and explain how you can use each to your advantage when dealing with horses. Understanding these inbred characteristics will unlock the secrets of horse behavior.

1. The Secret of Flight: The horse in its wild state depends upon flight as its primary survival behavior. The horse's natural habitat is grasslands, prairie or steppes. Its primary enemies in nature are the large predators, particularly those of the cat and dog family, such as lions and wolves. Anatomically, physiologically and behaviorally the horse is a sprinter. Considering its enemies and its habitat, sprinting straight away from any frightening stimulus is the best way for horses to survive. To understand horses, above all else, the natural instinct of this species to flee from real or imagined danger must be appreciated.

2. The Secret of Perception: Prey species must be more perceptive than predators if they are to survive. Horses are a prey species that live with the danger of being eaten by their predator enemies. They are programmed to be on the lookout for danger and are always prepared to flee from it in an instant. Inexperienced horsemen often fail to appreciate the extreme perceptivity of the horse. Horses have an uncanny ability to detect sensory stimuli which are far too vague for us to sense. We commonly interpret the flight reaction caused by the stimuli as "stupidity." Horses are incredibly aware of their surroundings, so much so that people often misinterpret the horse's reaction as "psychic" or the result of a "sixth sense." However, the responses, which elicit such opinions, are caused by reactions to the same five senses we possess: sight, hearing, smell, taste and touch. What is difficult for us to identify with is the superiority of those senses in the horse and the swift flight reaction that a stimulus to those senses can provoke.

3. The Secret of Response Time: The horse has the fastest response time of any common domestic animal. "Response time" or "reaction time" is defined as the ability to perceive stimuli and react to it. Prey species must have a faster response time than a predator or they get eaten. The horse is such a large animal that the speed of its response time is hard for us to comprehend. This short response time is essential in a flighty creature. It isn't enough to run away. One must run away *instantly* and at high speed to survive.

4. The Secret of Rapid Desensitization: The horse is more quickly desensitized to frightening stimuli than any other animal. Why is a flight-oriented creature so quickly desensitized to frightening but harmless stimuli? If this weren't so, horses would spend all their time running and there would be no time to eat, drink, rest, or reproduce. So horses, in nature, must quickly learn to ignore basically frightening but harmless things such as tumbleweeds, thunder, quail and other herbivorous prey species, such as bison, antelope, or deer. Once they learn, they never forget.

5. The Secret of Learning: Not only do horses desensitize faster than other domestic animals to frightening stimuli, but other kinds of learning are obtained with similar speed. If a novel experience, such as the first shoeing, the first trailer loading, the first saddling, the first worming, the first experience of any kind is traumatic, the horse will henceforth fear that procedure.

Conversely, if a novel experience is made pleasurable and if comfort rather than discomfort ensues, the horse will remember that and will be more accepting of such an experience in the future.

The reason that great trainers are able to obtain results with startling swiftness, is due to the fact that they use technically appropriate behavior shaping techniques in a species which is inherently able to learn with great speed - a matter of survival in a prey creature which depends upon flight to survive.

6. The Secret of Memory: The horse's memory is nearly infallible. Horses never forget anything! Fortunately, horses forgive and were it not for that fact, a majority of professional horse trainers could not make a living. Horses can and do survive inept, improper and inhumane training methods. Many of them manage to become satisfactory performers, although the information yielded by the relatively new sciences of ethology (scientific study of animal behavior in their natural surroundings) and behavior shaping show us that most of our traditional training methods are inefficient and cumbersome.

16

The donkey and its hybrid offspring, the mule, have as keen a memory as the horse, but unlike horses they do not forgive. Thus, donkeys and mules are notoriously more challenging to train than horses. All good mule trainers can train horses, but the reverse is not true. There is truth in the old saying, "Mules *must* be trained the way horses *should* be trained."

Horses categorize every learned experience in life as something not to fear and, hence, to ignore; or something to fear and, hence, to flee. This is extremely useful in the wild and utilizes the species' phenomenal memory, but it often creates problems in domestic situations. If a horse categorizes a harmless stimulus (such as an electric clipper, a piece of plastic, a white cat, a flag, a tractor, or a veterinarian, etc.) as something to run away from, it creates major problems to those of us who must handle it. What horses experience creates lasting attitudes, especially if the horses are young. It is incumbent upon those who must work with horses not to cause bad experiences that the horse will forever regard as a reason to flee. This makes it especially difficult for farriers and veterinarians because everything they do is frightening and some things are painful.

It is, therefore, the owners' responsibility to desensitize (train) horses to accept such routine procedures as farriery, veterinary examination including invasion of the body openings and basic therapeutic procedures such as dentistry, intubation, and oral or eye medication.

7.   The Secret of Dominance Hierarchy: The horse is the most easily dominated of all common domestic animals. It is a herd animal, subject to a dominance hierarchy and because it is a flight animal, the horse needs leadership to know when and where to run. In the wild, horses need leadership and readily accept it. Even naturally dominant individual horses (which are the exception in all animals that live in groups) can be dominated and rather quickly if one knows how to do it. The methods by which this can be accomplished most effectively are not natural to human beings. We must be taught.

8. The Secret of Control of Movement: The horse is the only common domestic animal that exerts dominance and determines the hierarchy by controlling the movement of its peers. It is understandable that in a species in which the ability to run away means life or death, positional control is the way in which leadership is established. Dominant horses make threatening movements towards subordinate herd members. The submissive individual, yielding its space, reaffirms the role of the dominant leader.

Control of movement is the basis of all horse training disciplines. Horses accept our dominance when we cause them to move when they'd prefer not to, or when we inhibit their movement. Thus, trainers use many techniques to control flight in the horse. These techniques include round pens, training rings, longe lines, driving lines, hobbles, lateral flexion of the head and neck, vertical flexion of the head, lateral control of the hind quarters, snubbing green colts to experienced horses and working them in harness next to an experienced horse.

9. The Secret of Body Language: Each species signals subordination or submissiveness with a body language instinctively understood by their own species. Horses give subtle signals when they are willing to submit to any domination. We must learn the body language of horses by experience or by education. As we shall see, the body language, or signalment, of horses is unique to the equine species. It is imperative that people handling horses learn to read the body language of their charges.

10. The Secret of Precocity: The horse is a precocial species, which means it is neurologically mature at birth. Commonly, the newborn of prey species is precocial. For example newly hatched chicks, ducklings, goslings, quail, grouse, newborn fawns, calves, lambs and foals are fully active soon after birth. Unlike kittens, bear cubs, puppies or newly hatched owls or hawks, all of which are predatory species and quite helpless at birth, the precocial species must be quickly able to recognize danger and flee from it.

The imprinting period of the precocial species is immediately postpartum, when they visualize and memorize what they see move and want to follow and respect it (which in nature is usually the mother). This helps them to stay with their dam and the herd and they are quickly imprinted to do so. In species with delayed imprinting periods this occurs much later (six or seven weeks in puppies, for example). These imprinting periods permit immediate learning and permanent retention. The best time to teach horses, therefore, is right after birth. Attitudes, temperament and reactions can be shaped in just a few hours if we know how.

Chapter 2

Understanding the Instinct to Flee

The primary defense of the horse is to flee from danger. Of all the common domestic animals, the horse is the only one in which flight is its main defense.

Each creature has a primary defense system and an examination of the anatomy of the species tells us what is the primary defense system. If we look at a dog, or one of its wild relatives such as the wolf, jackal, coyote, or dingo, we see teeth! When cornered, or when it feels its life is threatened, the dog will use its teeth. Cats, too, are powerful biters and most have a secondary defense weapon in their retractile claws. Although man has selectively bred some polled (hornless) breeds, wild cattle, sheep and goats all have horns which serve as their primary defense. Both male and female have horns that are acquired early in life. This tells us that horns constitute a primary defense tool. By contrast, in most species of deer, only the male has antlers and then only for part of the year. This tells us that the antlers are primarily intended for intra-species (within the herd) competition for territory and breeding rights. Deer, like horses, are primarily flight-defensive animals. The tusks of a hog, the horn of a rhinoceros, the camouflage coloration of the sage hen, the anatomical endowments of a skunk, a porcupine, an armadillo, or a tortoise, all reveal the primary defensive behavior of the respective animal when it feels that its life is threatened.

When we look at the horse, we are looking at a running machine. Its body is built for sprinting. Physiologically, its reaction time, its reflexes, its senses, its cardiovascular system, its respiratory system, are all designed to permit it to detect danger and to stay alive by sprinting away from it at high speed.

The horse, long ago, was a small, multi-toed, swamp-dwelling creature. Climatic changes resulted in swamps drying out to form prairies and savannas. The evolution of the horse allowed it to survive in this grassland habitat by running away from predators like large cats and wolves. Its limbs lengthened to facilitate speed. The number of its toes was reduced so that only one large central toe contacted the ground, permitting maximum escape speed. Vestigial toes remain in this incompletely evolved animal as ergots, chestnuts and splint bones.

The horse is physiologically, anatomically and behaviorally a sprinter. All three qualities are genetically transmitted, but all three can, within limits, be modified. Malnutrition or exercise can alter anatomy to some extent. Exercise or altitude can cause physiological changes. Training can shape or modify behavior. However, *all* of these changes are limited by the parameters of the specific species.

The flightiness of the horse is responsible for the high incidence of traumatic injuries in a domestic environment, to both horses and humans. It is the reason horses can be hard to handle, the reason it takes skill to train them, the reason horses can be dangerous and the reason many people regard them as stupid.

Horses are not stupid animals. Their behavior enabled them to survive in a hostile world. That world was a place of open grassy plains, not the domestic scene that we now require the horse to adapt to, filled with fences, barriers, confined places, noise, machines and crowds of people. It is amazing that this timid, flighty prey animal adapts so readily to the demands placed upon it by man. It is a tribute to such a creature that it has been successfully trained to pull wagons and combines, coaches and carts, charge and maneuver in battle, pursue bison and long-horned cattle, and quell urban riots. The horse has learned to jump fences that never existed in the wild and participate in parades with fluttering flags, drums and blaring musical instruments.

If the flightiness of the horse causes problems for us humans, we must also realize that this behavior also causes the horse to be so useful to us. For eons mankind merely hunted the horse as a food source. Five or six thousand years ago we domesticated the animal, herding it and selectively controlling its breeding. We channeled and directed the flightiness of the horse into the collar, into battle, after wild game, over fences, down the straight away, around the barrels, after the steer, out of the bucking chute, across the desert, up the mountain and down the polo field.

In doing these things, the horse made its way into the human heart to the point that the species has been lionized, glorified, deified and treasured by human cultures. If the dog is called, "Man's Best Friend," then surely the horse is "Man's Best Servant." Civilization marched behind the hoof prints of this animal and, until the twentieth century, without the horse, history would have been very different.

In managing other equine species, we sometimes err in assuming that the same principles and methods are suitable as those we use to manage the horse. This is not necessarily true. Donkeys and their hybridized offspring, the mule and the hinny, are similar in their behavior in many ways to horses. But horses evolved in grasslands that were swamplands that gradually dried out. The horse's anatomy changed to cope with this new environment. Its digestive systems had to adjust (with partial success, as we veterinarians know all too well) from a diet of succulent plants to one frequently consisting of dried grasses and grain. It grew larger and ran faster, its multiple digits evolved into a single digit most efficient on turf. Its flightiness increased and its response time decreased.

The donkey, on the other hand, adapted for the most part to arid, precipitous terrain. It became adept at thriving on sparse forage, withstanding high environmental temperatures, conserving moisture and at traveling long distances for forage or water. It also became far less flighty than the horse because, in the type of terrain most varieties of wild donkeys inhabit, blind flight could be disastrous. These animals, therefore, make a choice when they sense danger. They may run like a horse, or they may attack (this is the reason some sheepmen are using burros to defend flocks against coyotes), or they may simply freeze, refusing to move until they can analyze the danger and select the appropriate response. This is how the donkey or mule derives its legendary "stubbornness." If you're on a mountain ledge and see a lion in the distance, the best option may be to stand still. Mules, of course, being hybrids, may show either horse or donkey behavior. Anatomically and physiologically, they also show alternative characteristics.

So, here's the horse, a perceptive, flighty, *timid* creature whose main defense is to run away. This isn't its only defense, as we shall point out in a little while, but is its primary defense. More than any other familiar domestic animal, the horse wants to run from anything it interprets as a possible danger: a suspicious sound, a threatening movement, an unfamiliar odor, or the sight of any unfamiliar object, especially if it moves. The horse, although flighty, is a highly adaptable species. It learns fast, forgets nothing and its fear of unfamiliar things can be quickly overcome with the proper techniques.

Chapter 3

Understanding the Unique
Perception of the Horse

Perception is being aware of the things around us. The prey creature, to stay alive, *must* be more perceptive than the predator. Thus, the horse *is* a highly perceptive animal. Because it is the only one of our common domestic animals that depends primarily upon flight for survival, it is the *most* perceptive. Horses are more perceptive than we are because after all, we are a predatory, hunting species. It is difficult for a human to fully appreciate the perceptivity of a horse and we ought to consider this subject in some depth.

Horses, like us, have five senses. They are:

1. Sight - the visual sense
2. Touch - the tactile sense
3. Hearing - the auditory sense
4. Taste - the gustatory sense
5. Smell - the olfactory sense

Biologically, we are a hunting and gathering species. Our food is obtained during the day. At night we're supposed to huddle in caves, thus we don't have very good night vision. We are sight hunters and our eyes are well adapted to daytime hunting. Like hawks, owls, eagles, wolves and leopards, our eyes are in front of our head, so we have binocular, stereoscopic vision. This gives us excellent depth perception. We are very good at judging distances. Our focusing ability is remarkable. We can change the depth of our focus from a few inches away to infinity very quickly, especially if we are young.

Our hearing is relatively poor compared to that of a dog or a horse. They have a range of hearing that exceeds ours. Our sense of smell is far less than that of any of our domestic animals. We have a good sense of taste, but that sense has a small role in defense behavior in man or horse. Except for our fingertips, our tactile sense is inferior to that of a horse.

Horses are more perceptive than we are. We tend to underestimate horses' understanding of a situation because their perceptivity exceeds that of our own. When a horse detects some vague stimulus such as a sound of which we are unaware, an odor or a subtle hint of aggression in our stance, gait, voice, posture, or our demeanor, it often precipitates a flight reaction.

If the horse is unable to flee due to confinement or restraint, the flight reaction may manifest itself as panic, a violent attempt to escape, or by an alternate defense such as striking or kicking. The human response to such behavior is often to attribute it to stupidity or perversity.

Horses are not stupid animals. This flightiness and its associated perceptivity enabled the species to survive in a world full of giant lions, wolves, sabre-toothed tigers, hyenas and other predators. Indeed, *we* are stupid if we assign nature's remarkable adaptations to "stupidity." Any species capable of surviving and propagating in this hostile world has made intelligent adaptations to its environment.

1. Vision: More than any other sense, the vision of the horse is its primary danger sensor. It is the horse's vision with which we are least able to identify. In some ways the vision of the horse may seem to be inferior to ours. For example, horses have poor color vision. They see most things in shades of black and white and pastels. For that reason, black and white are the most visible colors to a horse, whereas for us it might be orange, yellow or red. That's why very black or very white objects are more frightening to a horse, especially if the object is unfamiliar.

Horses also lack our power of adaptation. Much of their focusing power relies not entirely upon an elastic lens which can change its shape as ours does, but upon a retina which is designed so that different parts of the retina clearly see things at specific distances. It's as if all horses wear trifocal lenses. This means that a horse approaching a jump, for example, must memorize the location and height of the jump, because the horse can't actually see the jump when it is close to it. This is also the reason that horses must cock their heads and arch their necks to see an object in front of them on the ground and why they will lower their nose and sniff the object to identify what they cannot clearly see.

Horses do not have our power of depth perception. Their eyes are set on the sides of their heads, the better to see predators sneaking up on them. Many prey species have lateral vision like this. Notice the eyes of rabbits, pigeons, chickens, deer and antelope. They all have laterally placed eyes with relatively poor depth perception. That is why a horse will panic at a wet spot on the ground. It can't tell if the puddle is one-quarter of an inch deep or 20 feet deep. The inside of a trailer is like an endless dark tunnel or cave. For horses in the wild, bad things come out of caves.

On the other hand, there are advantages in having eyes on the sides of one's head. There is a blind spot right in front and another right in back, but by the merest turn of the nose, the horse can see in back of it. In fact, by slightly turning its nose first one way, and then the other, horses can see all around them, 360 degrees. What an advantage that is when one's neighbors include lions and wolves. Of course, each eye sees a different view and each sends a different message to the brain. Those eyes have an incredible ability to detect movement. The horse can see a small bird flutter in a tree across a canyon. Movement may mean danger and danger, of course, means move the other way at top speed. No wonder horses get excited and nervous on a windy day.

The reason that horse's eyes "glow in the dark" is because of a special reflector in the eye called the *tapetum lucidum*. This structure greatly enhances the horse's ability to see at night. The horse's night vision, in fact, is so good that we cannot possibly identify with it. I've had horses carry me home on rocky canyon trails, without a misstep, when it was so dark that I could not see my hand in front of my face. A horse can sleep with its eyes open. Because the large predators hunt most often at night, we should always announce our presence when we approach a horse that is quietly standing with its eyes open. It may be asleep. Mature wild horses do not lie down to nap unless another herd member is serving as a sentry, scanning the surrounding area.

We humans have excellent powers of visual accommodation, especially when we are young. Our elastic lens quickly changes its shape allowing us to focus from near to infinity in a second or two. The horse has a relatively inelastic lens limiting its focusing power.

Not long ago I read a physiologist's description of equine vision in a horse magazine. The author made the statement that if a human had the vision of a normal horse "that person would be declared legally blind." I don't agree with that observation and I think that it completely underestimates the horse's ability to see things that we don't see and react accordingly. We have admitted earlier that the horse has limited color vision as compared to our own. Color-blind people are not considered legally blind.

The equine eye is uniquely able to detect movement. A horse does not miss the flutter of a bird hundreds of meters away across a canyon. The working cowhorse will see the movement of a range cow's ears hidden in the brush. Horses are nervous and flighty on windy days because moving vegetation may signify the approach of an enemy.

The remarkable memory of the horse compliments its superior vision. Horses remember everything. When their keen eyes detect a change in a familiar object, such as something new along a familiar trail, or if they detect a tiny movement in the grass, or in a wind blown bit of paper, that information immediately registers in the brain and sends a message: ALARM! POSSIBLE DANGER! PREPARE TO RUN! If some horses, especially older individuals, do not experience this alarm reaction, it is not because it wasn't perceived. It is because they have become desensitized or habituated to that particular stimulus. Without that ability, horses would be useless to us as working animals.

2. Touch: The tactile (touch) sense of the horse is important for us to appreciate. Only in our fingertips do we humans have the tactile sensitivity which horses have all over their body. Observe horses picking up solitary grains and blades of grass with their lips. What exquisite perception. Horses can feel a fly land on their hair (not the skin, but the hair). Think about that. Horses can feel the rider's most subtle changes in body position right through the saddle and pad. They easily detect changes in the rider's position which even the rider may not notice. The art of classical dressage is dependent upon conditioning the horse to respond to almost imperceptible signals conveyed by the rider's seat, legs and hands. All horsemen, regardless of their discipline, should study top dressage riders and their horses in action to gain an appreciation for the incredible tactile perceptivity of the horse.

The secret of great horsemen, whether they are jockeys, teamsters, or any kind of rider, lies in their awareness of the horse's response to tactile stimuli. Some people transmit confidence to horses with their hands, whereas others inspire anxiety. Second only to what they see, horses respond to what they feel.

This tactile awareness, combined with the athletic ability of the species has many implications. It is responsible for the powerful actions of the rodeo bucking horse. It explains much of the difficulty farriers and veterinarians have performing their procedures.

One aspect of this tactile sense can be successfully used in handling horses. After becoming desensitized to a tactile stimulus, horses like to be stroked. Of course, that's true of many species. Swine, dogs, cats and people enjoy stroking. Even birds and sea mammals display this behavior. It is especially pronounced in those species that engage in mutual grooming. Horses are mutual groomers.

The aware horseman, faced with a horse which displays fear from tactile stimuli such as grooming, shoeing, bridling, saddling, teeth floating and palpation can transform evasive behavior to welcoming behavior. In order to do this, the horse must be desensitized to a tactile stimulus which it previously interpreted as a threat. The stimuli must be presented as stroking.

As long as no pain is involved and appropriate behavior shaping techniques are used, horses can be taught to enjoy and welcome procedures such as grooming, foot trimming, floating teeth, palpation and even passage of a nasogastric tube. The behavior of horses who have learned to resist such routine procedures can be modified.

3. Hearing: The hearing of the horse is keener than ours, assisted by moveable ears. A horse can move one ear to face backward and have one ear forward to capture sound from all directions. They hear things we cannot and just as they memorize and categorize all visual stimuli which they encounter, they accurately memorize and categorize all acoustical stimuli. This is why a horse may be indifferent to one brand of electric clippers and panic when a new one is introduced. The new sound is a new ball game to the horse.

We've all noticed how dogs will recognize various car engines by their sound and know who is arriving. Horses can do the same thing. With such excellent hearing (and horses, unlike dogs, are not inclined to become

27

hard of hearing with old age), one realizes the folly that some horsemen engage in when using verbal commands to control the behavior of horses. For example, many people constantly cluck at horses to encourage forward movement. A single cluck is a command. It can serve as a very effective and readily available signal. But constant clucking quickly produces habituation. The horse hears it but no longer reacts to it. The sound soon serves as a form of displacement behavior to the person clucking.

Similarly, many riders say "Whoa!" when they want a horse to slow down. "Whoa!" should mean STOP completely and nothing else. Repeated "Whoas!" to slow a horse down or change its gait soon mean nothing. If a horse tosses its head while we are bridling it or examining its eyes and is otherwise standing still, why do we say "Whoa"? "Whoa!" means stop moving, not "hold your head still." Yet, when the horse doesn't comply with these confusing commands, the human's reaction is usually to decide that the horse is stupid.

4. Taste: We may decide that, given the horse's fondness for dry hay, wooden fences, bedding and lead ropes that it has an undiscriminating sense of taste. All we have to do is watch a horse graze in a pasture of mixed grasses to see how deftly it can select the more palatable species and reject those which are less palatable. It may even eat parts of the plant and reject other parts of the same plant.

Unlike cattle, horses are very particular about the taste of the water they drink. A change of water will often cause them not to drink. Many people who travel with competition horses bring the familiar water supply from home. Horses dislike stagnant, polluted, contaminated water or any water that is off-flavor. If there is an ingredient in a grain mixture they dislike, they will eat the preferred portions and leave the less palatable components behind. Yet, the sense of taste, although important to a horse, is insignificant compared to the other senses when it comes to precipitating a flight response.

5. Smell: The horse's sense of smell, like the dog's is so superior to ours that we cannot even begin to identify with it. Sound waves and odors, carried by the air, barrage the horse's mind. They often convey to the horse a message of danger. What must a horse smell on a windy day let alone what it sees and hears? Do rustling leaves and grass warn the horse that danger is sneaking up on it?

Horses often show alarm for "no reason." That's *our* interpretation. The horse's keen senses tell it that danger may be near and the horse's response to danger, always, is to run. If, in response to this kind of behavior, we become frustrated and angry, if we resort to the whip and the spur, what are we telling the horse? He's saying, "I'm afraid I will get hurt." If, indeed, we hurt the horse, his response is, "I *knew* that would hurt me and I'll be ready for it next time."

The key to the correct interpretation of the horse's behavior is understanding the world from its perspective. Its "world view" is based solely on its senses. The horse is motivated to seek either comfort or safety. It thinks it *must* flee in order to protect itself if it senses danger. A horse will not voluntarily tolerate discomfort very long. Continually responding to the horse in a manner that causes it more discomfort or threatens its sense of safety will always generate the thought of flight. The horse's perception is different from ours; therefore, we must know what to expect from the horse to understand the behavior of the horse.

Chapter 4

Understanding the
Horse's Response Time

Response time (also called reaction time) is the duration between the time it takes to perceive a stimulus (a baseball in flight toward your head) and the time you react to the stimulus (ducking out of the way of the ball). The horse has the fastest response time of any common domestic animal. This makes sense considering the fact that flight - the instinct to sprint away from perceived danger - is the horse's principal defensive behavior. This may seem surprising considering the size of the animal.

We all know how fast a dog can snap, a snake can bite, or a quail can burst into flight, but the response time (reaction time) of the horse is second to none. The interval between the time the horse's brain perceives a stimulus - feels a tactile stimulus, sees a visual stimulus or hears a sudden alarming sound and the time it sends a message to specific skeletal muscles to contract, is remarkably swift. Indeed, many experienced horsemen will testify that if a horse wants to strike or kick you the movement is so sudden that a human being cannot move fast enough to evade it. The horse's movement is often too fast to even be seen by the human eye.

Of all the competitive sports in which horses are used, none offers a more vivid example of this animal's lightning-fast response time than does cutting cattle. It is beneficial for all people, regardless of their preferred riding disciplines, to observe top-notch cutting horses in action in order to fully understand and appreciate the swiftness of the equine response after it has been thoroughly conditioned. For the uninitiated, it may be simpler to rent a cutting video. In fact, replaying such a video and watching the horses in slow motion may be the best way to see them.

31

Cutting horses are used to separate cattle from a herd - to "cut" one animal from the group. Cattle are herd prey animals and the one chosen to be cut does its utmost to return to the others. Trying to evade the horse, the cow will dodge, whirl and change directions at high speed.

A cutting horse in action. Notice that the horse is ahead of the action of the cow.

Photo by Don Weller ©1994

In competition, the rider is required to let the reins hang loose after the horse is shown the desired animal. The rider is not supposed to guide the horse's movements. Note that the cow initiates the maneuver. The horse has to see the movement, then respond to it and, by moving faster than the cow, block its attempts to get past the horse. The speed and the elusive footwork of the cow is usually no match for the faster movements of the well-trained horse, a vivid illustration of how much faster the equine response time is than the movements of even another prey species, a range cow.

Of course, training a horse to "cut cattle" takes time. Beginning with guiding the horse slowly, the horse's movements become completely conditioned responses. Yet, without an innately superior response time, no amount of training would enable the horse to outmaneuver the bovine.

The speed of the horse's response time can be seen elsewhere. Observe racehorses coming out of a starting gate. Watch good polo horses in action, or a well-trained rodeo roping horse follow a calf. Watch the heart-stopping maneuvers of a Rejoneador's horse in a bullfight. Again, the response time of the horse surpasses the extremely agile movements of the bovine.

It is recognized today that muscles carry varying proportions of slow-twitch and fast-twitch fibers. Athletes who excel in long distance prolonged activities have more slow-twitch fibers. Examples include human distance runners, wolves or hunting dogs that harry and exhaust their prey, and Arabian horses that excel in endurance races. The same thing is true of migrating species such as the Wildebeest and sled dogs that have remarkable endurance in long distance treks.

Other athletes, with a higher proportion of fast-twitch muscle fibers, excel in events that require great speed but which are of relatively short duration. Examples include human gymnasts and sprinters, hunting cats such as leopards and lions, and horses. Even though some horses, like the Arabian horse we mentioned earlier, have a relatively higher proportion of slow-twitch fibers than do most horses, they are still basically sprinters, varying only in the proportion of slow and fast-twitch fibers.

One breed of horse deserves special mention in this regard. The American Quarter Horse and those breeds in which an abundance of Quarter Horse breeding abounds, such as the American Paint Horse, the Appaloosa, the Palomino and the Buckskin breeds, have been selectively bred for a high proportion of fast-twitch muscle fibers. While this does not contribute to excellence in long distance events, such as endurance racing, it does create an even faster response time than naturally occurs in most horses. Thus, these breeds excel in sprinting, reining and cutting competitions.

It is fortunate that the breed has also been selectively bred for docility as well. Lacking this, the incredibly fast response time of this breed makes it potentially one of the most dangerous horses to work around. An ill-mannered, nervous, or aggressive Quarter Horse can move faster than most horses of other breeds and, therefore, can cause injury to itself or others more swiftly.

Quarter Horse registrations in the U.S.A. outnumber all other breeds combined. Today inept and inexperienced breeders breed many of these horses. Bred with horses of high speed racing bloodlines, such horses can be dangerous. It is important for Quarter Horse breeders not to overlook the qualities of mildness and tractability that the old-time breeders valued along with athletic prowess.

As society urbanizes and horses are increasingly owned by novice horsemen and kept in confined environments, we need gentler horses not flightier horses. It isn't enough to breed for performance and good looks. We must breed for temperament.

Chapter 5

Desensitization to Frightening Stimuli

It may seem inconsistent that the flighty, easily frightened horse can be more quickly desensitized to frightening sensory stimuli than other animals but, nevertheless, it is true.

What more vivid example can be given than the millions of horses that have been trained for military use? Horses have stood quietly in ranks under artillery barrage, charged into battle, carried knights in armor, pulled caissons, ambulances and supply wagons and were trained to lie down to provide cover for firing cavalry troopers.

Even today horses tolerate the banners and noise of parades; police horses calmly manipulate rioting mobs. Horses pack dead game for hunters. Buffalo and boar have been pursued on horseback. Some highly trained horses deftly avoid the charges of fighting bulls. In the ranching industry all over the world stock horses mingle with and control herds of half-wild cattle.

Surprisingly, horses can be quickly taught to tolerate such situations despite their innate qualities of flightiness, acute perception and swift reactions. How is this possible? It is possible because a creature that depends upon flight as its primary survival behavior *must* quickly desensitize to flight-provoking but harmless stimuli or it would be perpetually fleeing. There would be no time to eat, drink, rest or reproduce.

A beast armed with the formidable weaponry of a Cape Buffalo or a rhinoceros can afford to desensitize slowly. A brief charge can dispel most threats. Horses, however, must quickly learn when running is justified and when standing still is a safe alternative. Therefore, they can be taught to ignore stimuli as long as they are not harmed by those stimuli.

35

There are basically two methods by which this can be accomplished: *habituation* and *progressive desensitization*.

1. Habituation: Habituation is a technical term that means that the subject becomes desensitized to a specific stimulus to the point where it becomes oblivious to it.

Examples in our own lives might include a constant odor, such as that in a rendering plant, or a gasoline station. Eventually the worker no longer notices the odor. The sounds of a dripping faucet or a loudly ticking clock are examples of auditory stimuli we habituate to in our homes.

To habituate a horse to a potentially frightening stimulus we use a technique known as flooding. The horse, which must be closely confined so that it cannot escape, is vigorously and repetitiously exposed to the stimulus. Often in *less than one minute*, the horse which was originally terrified by the stimulus, will relax and soon ignore it.

The most common example of this technique in horse training is the "sacking out" of colts, a traditional part of American Western colt starting. The haltered colt, restrained by close confinement or hobbles, is repeatedly touched by a flapping sack or blanket until it quietly tolerates it all over its body.

In my videotape, *Influencing the Horse's Mind,* I demonstrate the sacking out of a green two-year-old colt using a noisy paper sack. The sack provides unfamiliar and, therefore, frightening visual, auditory, olfactory and tactile stimuli. The colt is unable to escape and very quickly settles down, becomes calm and soon ignores the flailing sack. In fact, since it is a form of stroking, he soon seems to enjoy it.

In flooding it is essential that the horse not be permitted to escape nor should the flooding process be stopped too soon. If either were to occur while the horse is attempting flight, or even thinking flight, then the flight behavior is reinforced. The next time the same stimulus is detected, the horse will resort to the same behavior that "made it go away" last time. This is exactly how so many evasive behaviors are caused in horses.

When habituating a horse to a stimulus, it is essential that the stimulus be repeated well past the point of habituation. One cannot offer too many stimuli, but to quit before complete acceptance occurs is a serious mistake.

Incidentally, many people inadvertently and unintentionally habituate horses to stimuli that they want the horse to respond to with an evasive reaction. An example is the rider who repeatedly and aimlessly prods the horse with his heels or spurs, sometimes at every step. The horse soon becomes habituated to this repetitious stimulus and no longer responds to it. The inept rider's solution to this situation is usually to kick harder or to buy bigger spurs.

How does one know when the horse is habituated to a specific stimulus? It no longer responds to it! It is no longer frightened by it! It ignores it! As said earlier, in most cases this can occur in less than a minute. But remember, to stop prematurely can teach the animal exactly the opposite of what we desire - to flee instead of quietly tolerating it. So, never hurry. Be patient and persistent.

Remember that horses, while they learn with remarkable speed and never forget a lesson, have little reasoning power. Therefore, a visual stimulus to which the left eye is habituated must be repeated for the right eye. Recent research reveals that horses *can* transfer learning obtained by seeing with one eye, to the other eye. (Hanggi, E. 1999 Interocular Transfer of Learning in Horses. *Journal of Equine Veterinary Science.* 19:2) Nevertheless, from a practical standpoint, it is important to visually habituate or desensitize horses by allowing them to see the object with both eyes. The object is literally a new object to the other eye. Any change means a "new ball game" for the horse. A sack of a different texture, size, shape, or shade is a new stimulus to the horse. If the entire body is desensitized to a currycomb, except for one spot, expect a fear reaction when that one spot is touched.

If the horse learns to tolerate one brand of electric clippers, do not be surprised if a different brand, emitting a different sound, elicits a flight reaction. To us it's just a different kind of clipper. To the horse it's a new and unfamiliar auditory stimulus.

2. Progressive Desensitization: The end result of this technique is the same as it is for habituation. What's the difference? It is done very slowly and progressively and it takes much longer. Why then, would one choose this method?

When the abruptness and fear induced by flooding might cause injury to either the horse or the handler (or both), it is much safer and more prudent to use progressive desensitization, even if the procedure takes much longer.

An integral part of progressive desensitization is the advance and retreat method. It is vividly illustrated in a video titled, *The Jeffery Method*. The late Maurice Wright, a fine Australian horseman, made the video. Wright was a protege of an earlier pioneer in equine behavior manipulation, a countryman named Kell B. Jeffery. Mr. Jeffery rejected the rough and tumble bronc busting methods of most Australian stockmen and developed a method of gently training previously unhandled horses. His technique largely utilized progressive desensitization and the advance and retreat method. Maurice Wright also authored the book, *The Jeffery Method of Horse Handling*. It is human nature, especially if we are male and more so if we are a young male, to advance and not retreat from an animal. That behavior enabled our species to survive in a hostile world. In working with horses, however, such behavior further intimidates an already fearful creature and further precipitates escape attempts. If escape is impossible, the horse is likely to take aggressive action.

So, if a frightening stimulus is presented to the horse such as the approach of a person and then, before a flight reaction occurs but is imminent, the person backs up a step or two, this aborts the flight reaction and relieves the horse's apprehension. Thus, we advance and retreat, advance and retreat, controlling our movements while observing the horse's tensing towards a flight mode. Each time we come just a little bit closer to the horse. If the fear is great, we retreat a bit farther. In a confined space we can eventually touch the horse and, if the method is done correctly, the horse eventually will become relaxed and indifferent to the touching. All this is done slowly.

Let me give a practical example. As a veterinarian, I routinely need to lift a horse's eyelids to examine the color of the mucous membranes of the eye. Many horses, already afraid of my appearance and the fact that I "smell like a vet" elevate the head beyond my reach - an evasive response. When I was young and foolish, my response to this was to pursue my objective more aggressively. This, of course, increased my patient's fear and, therefore, increased its evasive behavior. The answer, too often, was to apply a twitch to the horse's lip, an action that in itself ideally requires progressive desensitization.

I eventually learned (humans don't learn as fast as horses even though we are blessed with great reasoning power) to slow down, make myself less intimidating and, stroking the horse's face, use the advance and retreat method of approaching the eye. Gradually my hand would rub closer to the eye. If the horse showed fear, I'd retreat and rub farther from the eye.

Eventually, I could handle and manipulate the eye. Best of all, the horse enjoyed being handled, creating a safer situation for both of us, a more humane solution and usually one which promoted the confidence and respect of my client.

Chapter 6

The Fastest Learner

Intelligence may be defined in many ways. If reasoning power is part of intelligence, the horse must be rated very low. In fact, all species below man have little or no reasoning power. Keep in mind, however, that man seems to use his power of reason largely to justify his animal instincts. For example, we explain our desire to explore space with lofty goals, rather than admit that we, like most animals, are highly territorial and have always sought to acquire new territory. If we were to ask the educated leaders of the participants in political conflicts (such as Northern Ireland, the Middle East, Asia, or Africa) why they are willing to fight and even die for their cause, each side would give us rational justifications for their behavior. In reality, what motivates them are very primitive tribal and territorial instincts.

However, if intelligence is rated by qualities such as retention (memory), and speed of learning, then the horse must be considered extremely intelligent. Its memory often exceeds ours and its speed of learning nearly always does.

We have already discussed the remarkable speed with which horses can be habituated or desensitized to frightening stimuli. If correct techniques are used, desensitization to extremely frightening stimuli can often be observed within minutes. Later in this book we will discuss how a newborn foal may be lastingly habituated to an immense range of frightening sights, sounds, smells, and tactile stimuli in only an hour or two using flooding techniques. That is *very* fast learning.

In chapters to come we will describe learning techniques such as conditioned responses, counter-conditioning, and establishing ourselves as a herd leader without the use of violence, instead using subtle control of movement. The reason these techniques work so swiftly is not only

41

because they are appropriate teaching methods, but because the horse learns with such remarkable speed.

Again, an animal which has evolved by thoroughly using the survival behavior of sprinting away from perceived danger, *must* be a fast learner. The slow learners were the first to be eaten.

Comparing horses to dogs, which we all agree are very intelligent animals, may I point out that as a veterinarian I have known dogs that were hit by cars two or three times. How many times does a horse have to touch an electric fence in order to learn to avoid it?

How many people do you know who make the same mistakes over and over again? Will a horse do that? Intelligence is a subjective thing and if learning speed is one of the qualities by which we judge intelligence, the horse is a very intelligent animal.

Chapter 7

The Amazing Memory of the Horse

As a zoo practitioner, as well as a veterinarian for domestic species, I have often wondered why elephants are endowed with such a remarkable memory. Of any animal that I have worked with, elephants have the best memory. The horse, however, runs a close second. I don't know why this quality evolved in an animal that is so capable of defending itself as is the elephant, but an infallible memory is vital to survival for an animal like the horse which relies upon flight to survive.

Horses seem to remember every experience in life and they categorize each experience as something to tolerate with indifference (because it is harmless), or something to run away from. A bouncing, rolling tumbleweed? Ignore it! Range horses become thoroughly desensitized to tumbleweeds and learn not to react to them. A stalking lion? Run! Don't question! Run first! Analyze later!

Problems arise when horses characterize harmless things as something from which to flee. Examples include electric clippers, paper, or plastic sheeting, motorcycles, llamas, swine, anybody in a Western hat, or anybody driving a veterinary unit. When a keen memory is combined with an erroneous categorization, the result is a behavior problem.

It is important for those of us who associate with horses to fully appreciate how effectively they retain all sensory experiences and how quickly and lastingly they categorize them. The first incident of any kind experienced by a horse is important. The first veterinary treatment, the first shoeing, the first trailer ride, the first saddling - all leave an indelible impression upon the horse's mind and nothing short of a lobotomy will ever erase it.

Yet, undesirable behavior can be changed. It can be modified, but nothing will erase that first impression. We may be able to override misbehavior resulting from a bad first experience, but the memory of it will forever be in the back of the horse's mind, possibly to erupt in some future stressful situation.

It is better to make introductory experiences pleasant ones for the horse. The way young foals are handled, their attitude towards us and what we impose upon them is crucial to their future behavior. Being a precocial species, born with all of its senses fully developed, neurologically mature and having its critical learning times during the immediate postpartum period, the foal will remember every sensory experience and categorize them as things to tolerate, or things to flee, just as an older horse will. Appreciating this allows the horseman to understand the value of shaping the behavior of newborn foals.

Once again we see how a genetically predetermined behavioral characteristic (in this case memory) works in conjunction with the animal's primary defense which is flight. The rhinoceros or the Cape Buffalo needn't memorize and categorize every stimulus. If in doubt, charge! If the objective is harmless, all that's wasted is a bit of energy. If the objective is potentially harmful, the charge solves the problem. However, in the case of the horse, a sprint of several hundred yards is necessary to escape a threatening predator. Yet, the horse cannot run from every suspicious stimulus or there would be no time to eat, drink, rest, or reproduce. A horse must categorize each sensory experience. Therefore, it must have an extraordinary memory.

People who work with horses must understand and appreciate the memory of a horse for another reason. It is easy for us to misinterpret its completely logical reactions as stupidity or foolishness, even hostility.

For example, we ride along a familiar trail and the horse sees something that was not there last time. Perhaps it is a piece of paper, a puddle, a charred stump, an old refrigerator which some inconsiderate citizen dumped, or perhaps an old pair of jeans someone mysteriously left behind. If the object is white or black in color, it will elicit a more marked reaction, simply because those colors are more visible to an animal having poor color perception. To a greater or lesser extent, the unfamiliar object which, to the horse "doesn't belong there," will cause an alarm behavior. An older seasoned horse, which is trained to "follow" its rider and accepts that person as a leader and which has in its experience seen lots of such frightening objects may merely direct its ears and eyes towards them. The desire to flee may express itself by a tensing of the body and a snort. At the other extreme, a green, young and inadequately trained horse may shy, whirl, or run off. It is important to understand that it is not perversity that causes horses to act this way. It is fear and fear motivates this species to run.

What does the horse fear? It fears injury. Horses shy when they perceive something that they remember as being threatening, or when they perceive something that their memory tells them doesn't belong there. They're afraid that it will hurt them.

So what do most trainers teach the rider to do when a horse shies and "stupidly" attempts to flee something it perceives as dangerous? They insist the rider force the horse to face what it thinks might hurt it, using the whip and the spur. The horse is telling us, "I'm afraid I'll get hurt!" So we hurt it! This serves to confirm the horse's fear and this is the reason so many horses habitually shy.

Does this make sense? Of course not! When a horse shows fear of harmless stimuli, all we need do is use the previously described techniques of habituation and desensitization to dispel the fear and then use positive reinforcement (something pleasant like a food treat or brief petting) to make the frightening object a desirable object. Horse behavior is easily shaped or modified, *if* the correct techniques are used.

When we persist in using improper techniques, even if they come more naturally to us because of our instinctive, predatory behavior, then getting the horse to do what we want may take many hours, weeks or months. Frequently, we will fail altogether, usually satisfying ourselves that the horse is stupid, obstinate, or a poor learner.

Chapter 8

The Dominance Hierarchy

Animals that live in herds or groups, such as cattle, dogs, wolves, antelope, baboons, chickens, whales, dolphins, gorillas, turkeys, goats, humans and horses have a dominance hierarchy. Creatures that are basically loners, such as most species of cats and bears, also have an order of dominance when they occupy shared territory, but the hierarchy is not as important as it is in those species in which numbers enhance the probability of survival. For example, wolves and dogs are pack hunters. Their predatory success is improved when they hunt in groups. Alone, when game is scarce, they are more likely to starve. The same thing is true of primitive man. Primitive humans were pack hunters, best able to insure a food source by means of cooperative hunting and food gathering. This is the reason that dogs and humans so easily bond. To the dog we are a surrogate pack. To the human, the dog is a clan member. Both are pack hunters. Each is endowed with genetic attributes that add to the effectiveness of either species and help to assure survival in a challenging habitat.

The order of dominance within the herd is established by behaviors. Ultimately, a hierarchy is determined within the horse herd with a leader at the top and increasingly subordinate herd members below that ranking member.

In wild horse herds, or in feral bands as in the American Mustang, or the Australian brumby, the leader is usually an older mare. A stallion owns the herd, but it is led by a dominant older mare often so old as to be decrepit. She maintains her role with assertive, dominating behavior when in fact she may be physically weaker than most of the other horses.

47

Why does an older mare lead the herd? The answer is obvious in prey species whose primary defensive behavior is flight and which depends upon its keen senses of perceptivity, fast response time and reliable memory. The older mare has had the most experience. She has categorized more incidents, has had more close encounters and survived more threats than any of the younger members of the herd. She knows when to run, which direction to run and how far to run. When the band is in flight she leads (even if she isn't in the front) and customarily the stallion runs behind urging the laggards to keep up.

Thus, it is not gender but seniority that determines the leadership of the group combined with natural assertiveness and leadership qualities. The best evidence that this is true is seen in domestic range herds in which the leadership is sometimes assumed by a gelding. In fact, I have seen range herds absolutely ruled by a Shetland Pony gelding. Any horse in the groups could probably have killed these little geldings, but their assertiveness was irresistible. Size does not determine dominance among horses otherwise humans could not dominate their mounts.

In nature there are no old stallions leading horse herds because as soon as a stallion is past his prime, a younger and more aggressive stallion displaces him. Mares normally cycle reproductively throughout their lives. They do not go through a menopause. Old mares persist within the breeding band until eliminated by infirmity. At that point, unable to keep up, they are usually eaten by predators. It is experience that is so valuable to the group. A mare that has survived to old age has done so with a combination of luck, awareness and unhesitating flight when flight is called for.

From the standpoint of horsemanship there is tremendous significance to all this. It means, first of all, that all horses can be dominated. Even the most naturally dominant individual - an ALPHA - can be dominated. It's just a question of knowing how to do that.

Dominating a horse isn't a matter of whips and chains. It does not imply or require physical abuse or the infliction of pain. If an old mare can lead a horse herd comprised of a stallion, younger mares and yearling stallions, it should be obvious that the requirement for the leadership role is not physical strength. If it were could any human rise to the top of a horse's hierarchy? Could a slip of a girl, a child, or a senior citizen obtain the performance possible from a well-trained horse? Could Johnny

In a true demonstration of leadership, Silka Valentin, a young German woman paralyzed from the waist down, has gained the respect of her 1600 lb. Friesian, Biko. Using the natural horsemanship methods of Pat Parelli she is able to lead and ride her horse. *Photos courtesy of Debby Miller.*

Longdon or Willy Shoemaker or any professional jockey lead their young and powerful mounts to victory?

To understand the behavior of the equine species, the concept of the dominance hierarchy is second in importance only to the appreciation for the flightiness of this timid prey animal. Those who work with horses must comprehend the fact that complete control of this large and swift creature is only possible by assuming a leadership role. That means that the horse regards us as above it in the dominance hierarchy and the higher it sees us, the more compliant the horse. The more *respectful*, to use the horseman's language.

But it is also essential to realize that achieving this role does *not* require the infliction of pain or cruel or inhumane tactics. It is necessary for the horse to respect us and not to fear us. There is a difference between respect and fear. The difference is in attitude. A horse that respects a human will submit because it recognizes its place in the heirarchy. A horse that fears a human will obey a command purely out of fear that it will get hurt. Its primary motivation is to avoid getting hurt, not to submit. A student that submits to authority is much easier to work with. A student that is fearful of getting hurt isn't really isn't learning anything other than how to avoid getting hurt. It appears as though the horse is obeying, but the motivation or attitude of the horse is negative rather than positive. We hopefully respect our parents, but we should not fear them. We may respect our teachers, but we should not fear them. We ought to respect law enforcers, but if we are law abiding, it shouldn't be necessary to fear them. Unfortunately, because so many of us lack the qualities necessary to be inspired leaders, many parents, teachers and law-enforcement officials do elicit fear from their charges rather than respect. So do many horsemen.

Historically, a majority of horsemen cause fear rather than respect in the horses they work with. Emotions such as anger, frustration and impatience cause behavior in humans that intimidate horses. Horsemen who cannot contain their emotions, who lose their temper and force their own ineptness upon the horse evoke fear, not respect.

In 1889, Captain M. H. Hayes, a British army veterinary surgeon, wrote one of the best books ever written about horses and horsemanship, *Illustrated Horse Training*. He observed that the qualities necessary to be a truly great horseman are the qualities which define the best in human nature: knowledge, patience, resourcefulness, sympathy, skill, coolness and pluck.

To gain the respect of a horse we need those admirable qualities. To obtain fear, to have the horse regard us as a predator, rather than as a leader, all we have to do is have temper tantrums and substitute violence and cruelty for kindness and understanding. What a noble challenge the horseman faces.

Chapter 9

The Body Language of the Horse

In the battle for the order of dominance within the group, each species has developed a body language that signals either assertiveness or submissiveness. This body language is not learned. It is instinctive behavior and it is different for each species because each has evolved in different ways to survive in a given habitat. It is, like the anatomy and the physiology of the given species, genetically predetermined. Within certain parameters these characteristics are flexible.

For example, our anatomy as a species is genetically predetermined. We know that a human baby will look human when it is born and not like a frog, a stork, or a bear.

However, if we are nutritionally deprived as a child, it may alter our anatomy. Our height may be stunted or our limbs deformed. If we lift weights regularly our anatomy will be changed. All of these changes are within limits determined by our specific species.

Physiologically, we may vary if we live at very high altitude, if we run five kilometers every day, or if we are afflicted with a metabolic disease. Yet the variations are within the limits for our species.

Similarly, the behavior of any individual is basically determined by the genetic code for the species, yet it can be shaped, within limits, by environmental factors. A dog urinates on trees and posts to mark his territory. That is not learned behavior. It is instinctual. But we can teach the dog not to urinate in the house. That is learned behavior. Chasing livestock is a genetically predetermined behavior in Border Collies. Controlling the direction and duration of the chase is learned behavior.

The signals by which animals establish a dominance hierarchy within a group are natural behavior for that species. It isn't taught but it is automatically understood by that species. This is a very important concept because, as we shall see, it enables man to quickly communicate with and dominate his domestic animals, providing that he has learned their language.

Assertive behavior in each species is related to the anatomical defense nature has provided. We can predict the behavior of aggression or defense simply by looking at the anatomy of the animals.

Consider the behavior of a threatened porcupine, skunk, armadillo, turtle, rhinoceros, wild boar, leopard, wolf and a bison. In each case the primary defense weapon is obvious. In the case of the horse, as we have abundantly pointed out, we see a sprinter. Its body and behavior are designed to survive by running away from danger. Thus, each species when threatened displays its defensive endowments.

The dog snarls and shows its teeth. The bovine lowers its head and presents its horns. The horse assumes a sprinting position: head up, back rounded, haunches gathered - much like a human sprinter in the blocks. It's the body posture so many horses assume the moment they identify me as a veterinarian.

Conversely, each animal, to signal submissiveness, assumes a position of vulnerability for that species. I have observed these behaviors in our common domestic animals.

What does the dog do to signal submissiveness to the dominant individual in the group? It lies down and exposes its throat and belly, saying, in effect, "Go ahead. Kill me. I won't defend myself."

What do humans do? The opposing thumb and erect posture of our species are the anatomical clues to our primary defense. We raise the closed fist, holding a symbolic club, our primary defense for hundreds of thousands of years (until we eventually learned to sharpen it, throw it and call it a "spear"). In all human cultures, the threat of the upraised fist is instinctively understood. So how do we signal submissiveness? We present the back of our head to the club. We bow our heads. In all cultures a bowed head is an act of submission. Thus, we bow to superiors, bow to royalty, bow in prayer and bow to the deity. Whether we bow deeply, nod our head, or prostrate ourselves like a Moslem is determined by culture, but bowing the head is an instinctive submissive signal in our species. We also nod "yes" in acquiescence.

When are horses most vulnerable? When they are eating or drinking. With its head down, a horse cannot use its keen senses of vision, hearing, or smell to its best advantage. That's why the lion waits at the water hole. With bad footing in the mud and its head down, a zebra or a wild horse is extremely vulnerable.

So what does the subordinate horse do when confronted by the dominant herd member? It simulates eating or drinking. It lowers its head position and it chews and licks its lips. Submissive behavior is most dramatically displayed in the very young. Their small size makes them more vulnerable and they know it. Puppies will most frequently roll over when approached and little foals will "snap" or "pop" their lips when approached by a human or another horse. We only understand the body language of our own species. Unless we learn that of another species, we are incapable of understanding what they are saying.

Inexperienced horse owners will often complain that a newborn foal is trying to bite them when, in fact, the foal is anxiously opening its lips with its head and neck extended, trying to say, "Please don't hurt me. I'm just a helpless nursing baby." To the uninformed humans that behavior resembles the aggression of the more familiar dog.

The head position and mouth expression of the horse, therefore, signal the horse's decision to accept another individual as dominant, whether it is a horse or human. The head will be lowered and the lips will be smacked and licked to signal submissiveness. The lowering of the head may be very subtle. It will perhaps be lowered very slightly and only momentarily if the horse is unsure about conceding its role in the dominance hierarchy. On the other hand, the movement may be very exaggerated if the horse is overwhelmed by submissiveness. These head movements can be seen most dramatically in the round pen starting technique so popular with most of the trainers who are now doing public clinics for horsemen. *Join Up,* a videotape produced by Monty Roberts, is especially expressive. He starts a Thoroughbred colt in the round pen, causing a flight response. After the colt has gone its genetically programmed flight distance, it starts to signal surrender by dropping its head and licking its lips. Mr. Roberts persists in causing it to flee, occasionally switching directions (control of movement, to be discussed later), until it is bowing so strongly that its nose contacts the ground. He then assumes a passive position and non-aggressive stance, whereupon the grateful colt, head lowered and licking its lips, immediately comes up to him and follows wherever he goes, completely accepting his leadership. The body language exhibited by the horse is of special interest in this video.

The act of the green horse called "reaching for the bit," is a stage that most trainers watch for realizing that a certain plateau has been reached. I believe that this is nothing more than a biological signal of submission. It occurs in the round pen devoid of bit or bridle and similarly occurs when the young horse is worked and bitted, whether under saddle, at liberty, on the longe line, or when driven. It does indeed indicate a plateau. It is a signal of submissive acceptance. Similar behavior can be observed within a group of horses in a pasture or in wild mustangs even when human presence is lacking.

Chapter 10

How Leadership is Established

We have described how each species is endowed physically with defensive capabilities that determine the primary defensive behavior of that species. Dogs snarl, show their teeth and snap. Cattle lower their heads, present their horns and charge. Horses elevate the head and neck, dilate the nostrils and gather their muscles to whirl and sprint away.

In each species (this is my personal observation, not an established scientific fact), if the primary defense is controlled, the individual is defenseless and will usually recognize its helplessness. It will eventually signal submission.

If a dog's mouth is tied shut, aggressiveness will usually convert to frantic submissive behavior which, in the dog, is manifested by a lowering of the body position, urination and expression of the anal glands.

Dog training halters that do not have a collar to go around the neck, utilize a head collar or halter. (The Gentle Leader® Premier Pet Products, Richmond, Virginia) When the leash is tugged, it momentarily closes the dog's mouth and works on the principle of controlling primary defense behavior. Actually, dogs and wolves, when competitively jousting often employ this technique, momentarily grasping the opponent's muzzle in their own teeth and applying pressure. This symbolically says, "I close your mouth! I take away your defense! I am in charge!"

We control cattle by controlling the head. Using nose tongs, a bull ring, or a stanchion or headgate, we deprive the animal of the use of its main weapon, its horns. Such a means of restraint could not be used for dogs or horses or many other species, but it is quite effective for cattle.

Swine are restrained with a loop of wire or a cable around the snout, behind the tusks. The tusks! The only visible weapon in swine!

Law enforcement officers know that when an aggressive prisoner is handcuffed behind his back submission usually ensues. In humans the hands are the primary weapons of defense.

Perhaps the above observations merit challenge, but there is no question about the validity of the concept as it applies to horses. They are the only one of the above-mentioned species in which flight - movement - is the key to survival in the wild.

Movement is life to the horse. Control the movement of the horse and you can control its mind. Control its mind and you can control its behavior. Every horse training method ever devised relies upon control of movement as the key to controlling behavior.

Movement can be controlled in two ways:

1. We can inhibit movement when the horse would prefer to move.
2. We can cause movement when the horse would prefer to be still.

In either case, the horse will eventually become submissive to us. It will search for help and look for a herd leader to show it the way out of a dilemma. This submissive behavioral change is signaled by means of the body language.

Let us now consider practical applications of each of the two methods of controlling movement.

1. Preventing Movement (Flight Control): The horse's instinct is to escape a perceived threat by sprinting away from it in a straight line if the terrain permits it. Controlling this capability causes submissiveness. An example of this is halter breaking. If a horse is properly halter broken (and not all are), the animal is compelled to follow the lead rope and to stand when tied. The horse that is properly trained will undergo a visible behavior change when haltered. A vivid example of this phenomenon, familiar to every equine veterinarian, is the aggressive broodmare with a newborn foal. Some of these mares are extremely aggressive, yet, after being caught and haltered, most show an abrupt change in demeanor. Aggressiveness changes to concern and anxiety and they become more submissive and compliant to the handler.

Green horses are often started by being snubbed to an older, schooled horse, or they are harnessed next to an experienced driving horse. In North America and in other parts of the world, old time bronco riders often tied up a hind leg. The effect is not just to inhibit kicking. It helps to render the horse psychologically submissive by limiting its mobility. The same effect can be observed by hobbling one foreleg. John Rarey, the best known of the nineteenth century American "horse tamers," primarily used a single foreleg hobble to subdue outlaw horses. Other famous horsemen used this method as well as other means of controlling flight during the last century. D. Magner used a head-to-tail tie. The horse, attempting flight, could only circle helplessly until it became meekly submissive.

It has long been known that casting a horse, causing it to lie helplessly on its side, causes a profoundly submissive attitude.

Teaching young horses to tolerate hobbling is, I believe, an important part of the schooling. This should include the immobilization of each of all four legs separately and also the use of two leg hobbles on each pair of legs. This not only creates an attitude of respect for the trainer, but it also teaches the horse to compliantly yield its legs. This is not only helpful to the farrier, but also greatly reduces the probability of a disastrous outcome if the horse should ever become ensnared in wire, rope, or in a fence.

Horsemen will often suggest to the veterinarian that an equine patient be handled in its stall rather than outside. Why should a horse be more cooperative in its own territory than outside of the stall? The horse knows that it cannot escape from the stall and is, therefore, more submissive.

When doctoring horses, the use of stocks usually produces a more relaxed and compliant patient, assuming that the horse is properly trained to a stock. When palpating broodmares, most equine practitioners have noted that the patient is more relaxed in a chute than if palpated in the open.

Blindfolding horses has long been used as a means of restraint. Why is it effective? The blindfolded horse does not know which way to run. Flight is therefore inhibited.

Early in training, competent horse trainers establish lateral flexions of the head and neck as a conditioned response. Again, this inhibits the flight response. Similarly, a rider establishes control of the hindquarters so that the hindquarters can be displaced laterally (disengaged) in response to the rider's leg pressure. Because the horse's propulsive power comes from its hindquarters, the ability to move forward, rear, or to buck is compromised when they are moved laterally.

Later the skilled rider will seek vertical flexion of the head and neck. Although horses can run with the head flexed vertically, the normal sprinting position for the species is head up, nose extended.

An excited horse, ridden persistently in circles, will eventually become less agitated, not because it physically tires, but because it realizes that its efforts have not accomplished its goal - which is to escape. Most trainers utilize this technique.

Young horses, securely tied for many hours, may fret initially, but eventually they become resigned and placid. Trainers attribute the improved behavior to "patience," but what has actually caused the behavior change is submissiveness after the horse realizes that escape via flight is not possible.

2. Causing Movement: Many other methods of schooling horses utilize the principle of forced movement to establish leadership over the horse. Examples include longeing, driving and the increasingly popular use of a round pen for liberty work. The principle of flight control is at work because even though movement is encouraged it is confined and directed. This is quite different from the horse's natural desire to escape perceived danger by sprinting directly away from it.

It is interesting to note that the signalment of submission by the horse - lowering the head and licking the lips and chewing movements - can be produced by either causing motion or, conversely, by inhibiting it. A horse with one foreleg doubled and held in flexion with a strap or rope hobble will eventually signal submission. The same horse, put into a round pen and caused to gallop endlessly by using an intimidating stimulus such as a longeing whip or a flag will finally begin to bow its head and work its mouth, pleading for help. When allowed to rest that horse will, ironically, approach the handler who has been frightening it and with submissive body language ask for that person to assume the role of herd leader.

Chapter 11

A Precocial Species

Konrad Lorenz, an Austrian scientist, was the founder of modern ethology (the science of comparative behavior). Prior to World War II, he described his experiments with newly hatched Greylag Geese which would accept and follow, as real or foster parents, whatever they first saw when they emerged from the egg. Lorenz called this phenomenon "imprinting," and it was soon apparent that it occurred in many species. Lorenz observed that the initial imprinting affected subsequent adult behavior and proposed that each species is genetically constructed to learn specific kinds of information early in life which is important for the survival of that species. The imprinting period and other critical learning periods are windows of opportunity where humans can beneficially shape the behavior of domestic animals.

Having worked with horses since I was quite young, I had always been told that to handle a newborn foal was to risk its rejection by the mare because of the human smell on the foal. This handling would further damage the newborn by spoiling it. This was a common belief in North America and other parts of the world.

However, after a few years of veterinary practice, I observed that the foals that I was forced to handle at birth, usually for obstetrical reasons, were gentler and more docile than those that had been handled minimally. Moreover, the foals seemed to remember me, even weeks later and many seemed to desire my company. Suspecting that imprinting was involved, I began to experiment with my own foals handling them deliberately and extensively at the time of birth.

Foals are precocial. Like many prey species, they are born small but fully developed. They are neurologically mature and all of their senses are fully functional, as is the case with members of the sheep, goat, cattle,

61

deer and antelope families. Birds such as geese, ducks, chickens, quail and pheasant are also fully functional at hatching. This is in contrast to the offspring of most predators, in which the newborn are quite helpless and immature. Consider newborn human babies, cats, dogs, bears, hawks, eagles, or owls. The reason for precocial development in prey species is obvious. The young must, as soon as possible, be able to recognize and follow the mother in order to stay alive.

The significance of this is that the newborn foals are precocial and are not only fully capable of learning immediately after birth, but actually have enhanced learning capabilities at this time. The imprinting time for the horse is immediately after it is foaled and within the critical learning times which are within the first few days. The critical learning times for puppies and kittens are six to fourteen weeks of age. Just as a child learns to speak during a specific critical learning time and is capable of learning several languages simultaneously each with a specific dialect (care to try to do that after you are grown?) the very young foal can swiftly and lastingly learn an unlimited amount of information. This early learning will, as in any species, permanently shape its adult behavior and its attitudes.

Considering these facts, it is obvious that training the newborn foal is the fastest and most effective as well as the most convenient method of teaching horses. Conversely, adverse experiences, including imitating the behavior of an ill-mannered mare, can adversely shape the future behavior of the foal.

Initially, because I am a veterinarian, my primary efforts were directed towards the *desensitization* of the newborn foal. This process would allow it to tolerate examination, invasion of its body openings, manipulation of all parts of its body and accept such potentially frightening equipment such as electric clippers, sprayers, bandages, nasogastric tubes and dental instruments.

Eventually I added *sensitization* techniques to control the position of the foal. These included moving in any direction in response to light pressure. I found that, in less than one minute per procedure, I could teach a foal to move forward, back up, move laterally and yield either forehand or hindquarters. This learning was retained even weeks later. These controlled movements exert a dominating effect upon the foal. Repeatedly causing and controlling motion in horses creates respect and acknowledgment of our role as a herd leader.

Therefore, desensitization of the newborn foal produces a calm, steady horse and sensitization to certain stimuli creates a respectful, willing horse.

Because learning is so quick and so lasting in the foal, it is vitally important that the training be performed correctly. It is better not to handle the foal at all than to do it improperly. Imprint training, because it is done during the imprinting period as soon as possible after foaling, is easy to do. Even a novice can do it effectively, but it is essential that the procedure be understood and performed correctly for the best results. When done correctly, it is one hundred percent effective in all breeds of horses and is equally effective in other equine species such as mules and donkeys. Even zebras have been imprinted successfully. During the last ten years, as my method became internationally popular, many people who had heard about imprinting but who had never been fully instructed in it did not fully understand the process, began to handle their newborn foals. Unfortunately, some of these foals were mishandled, causing poor results. Most commonly, in desensitizing the foals that happened to have strongly dominant and stubborn personalities, the job was hurried. Applying an inadequate number of stimuli and stopping when the foal still desires to flee will produce a lasting flight effect, exactly what we are trying to extinguish.

When I first developed this method, attention was concentrated only on desensitization to frightening stimuli and sensitization was ignored. The foal that is desensitized and not taught to respond with movement to specific signals will lack respect and submissiveness and later on will act "pushy" and "spoiled."

Ignoring my warnings, many owners will allow the foal to nibble at their fingers or clothing or otherwise act disrespectfully.

The most important things for a foal to learn from us when it is being trained are:

- *I can touch you, but you may not touch me without my permission.*
- *I can invade your personal space, but you must not invade mine unless invited to do so.*
- *I can put my fingers in your mouth, but you must never put your mouth on me.*
- *I can touch your feet, but you must never put your feet on me.*

- *I can cause you to move in any direction, but you must never cause me to move.*
- *I can control your movement and prevent you from moving. When haltered, you must never pull back and you must follow where I lead.*
- *When requested, you must willingly follow me anywhere I want to go, even when I am on your back.*
- *You will like me, trust me and willingly accept my leadership*

Obviously, such a contract obligates us as well as it does the horse. It is incumbent upon us never to lose patience, never to lose our temper and to always be just and kind. If we break that contract, then the horse is justified in doing likewise.

Chapter 12

Training Newborn Foals

Earlier we discussed two methods by which horses can be desensitized to frightening stimuli. These were habituation (flooding) and progressive desensitization.

Horses of any age can be quickly habituated to very frightening stimuli. To desensitize a horse via progressive desensitization takes a much longer time than using a flooding technique to habituate it to the same stimulus. For example, to habituate a horse to having an ear handled can be done in less than a minute by flooding the restrained horse. To accomplish the same thing with a progressive "advance and retreat" technique may take a long time, perhaps as long as half an hour.

Why then, would anyone choose the slower method? The reason is that flooding the horse rapidly may be dangerous. The frightened horse may injure itself in a desperate attempt at flight (and such reactions keep veterinarians busy repairing the ensuing injuries). Or, unable to flee, the horse may resort to a fight reaction and injure the person training it (and such reactions keep physicians busy repairing the ensuing injuries).

The single greatest advantage in desensitizing foals as soon as possible after birth is that the flooding technique can be used to completely desensitize the foal *permanently*. It can become desensitized to having any part of its body handled, to electric clippers, plastic, paper, loud noises, sprayers, dogs, pigs, cattle, bells, flags and whistles. All of this can be done in an average time of one hour, although some strong-willed, dominant, or highly reactive foals may take as long as two hours. *The important thing is to persist in the flooding stimulus until complete habituation occurs.* If we stop too soon, while the foal is thinking flight, we will fix the flight reaction and instead of desensitizing the foal to the stimulus being used we will have sensitized it. We will have rewarded the thought of flight.

This foal, only a few hours old, is being desensitized using a white plastic bag. Notice the soft look in its eye as it accepts the flooding techniques.

Photo courtesy of Debby Miller.

We cannot do too many stimuli when flooding the foal, but we can do too few. The safest route then, especially for the novice or inexperienced handler, is to use a lot of stimuli and these are most effectively done rapidly and rhythmically. For example, if we are trying to desensitize the foal's nostrils so that it will calmly tolerate the passage of a stomach tube some day, we introduce a finger into the nostril and wiggle it repetitively and rhythmically. At first the foal will struggle, wanting to run away (even if it has been just born and has never been on its feet). After twenty, thirty or forty stimuli the struggling will cease. The foal will relax. Then it will become almost mesmerized by the repetitious stroking within its nostril. The point of habituation has been reached, but don't stop then. Continue the flooding for a while to be sure that it is completely past the flight response. That nostril (and only that nostril) is now permanently desensitized to a probing finger, but not yet to a tube. A transition must be

66

made to the tube, but that transition has been greatly facilitated by what we have done. Indeed, a small nasogastric tube can be used to further desensitize the foal if desired.

I gently insert my finger into the foal's nostril and wiggle and move it around to desensitize the nostril. Later on, this will help the foal accept a tube that is inserted through the nostril to reach the stomach.

Photo courtesy of Debby Miller.

The same approach is used to desensitize all body openings and all areas which will, in the future, be extensively handled. Remember to persist in the stimulus beyond the point of acceptance. If you quit while the foal is resisting, you have taught him it is okay to resist the procedure. The following is a list of body parts that benefit from desensitizing:

- The head: neck, ears, eyes, face, both nostrils, mouth, tongue.

67

- Saddle area: girth or cinch area, top of back, complete underside of foal.
- Perineum, tail, anus (use surgical glove with lubrication).
- Each leg entirely and feet (especially the bottom of feet to simulate farrier work).

I am desensitizing this foal's ears by repeatedly and rhythmically handling the inside and outside of the ear. I continue the handling until the foal is completely ignoring my touch.

Photo courtesy of Debby Miller.

The foal, properly desensitized as soon as possible after foaling, is a pleasure for the farrier, the veterinarian, or the trainer to work with later on.

In a videotape I made titled, *Early Learning,* desensitizing two newborn foals is shown in complete detail, followed by the sensitizing procedures. All of these "imprint training" procedures are also thoroughly described and well illustrated in the book, *Imprint Training of the Newborn Foal.*

Establishing Conditioned Responses in the Foal: While the foal is lying down and we are performing the desensitizing procedures, we can also do certain things which will profoundly affect its future behavior. We can teach it to yield its head and neck and to yield its legs. This is easily accomplished and will help to establish conditioned responses.

Turn the foal's head to the side until its nose approaches its withers and gently hold it there until resistance is gone. This may take several minutes in some foals. If this is done in both directions, to the left and to the right, the foal will have learned to yield the head and neck laterally. This is why these foals can be so quickly taught to lead as soon as they are on their feet and well coordinated. I teach them to lead at one or two days of age and it only takes a few minutes. Moreover, when the horse is old enough to be ridden or driven, it will quickly respond to the rein because it learned to yield the head laterally soon after it was born.

Similarly, when handling the newborn foal, flex each leg completely and hold it in sustained flexion until long after all attempts to straighten the leg are gone. The foal will have learned to yield its feet and legs. This is in addition to the rubbing and stroking of the entire leg in order to desensitize it and in addition to the repeated tapping of the hooves in order to accustom it to shoeing.

There is an important side benefit to teaching the foal that it must yield its head, neck and feet to us, compliantly and quietly. As I have previously pointed out, the dominance hierarchy in the equine species is established by control of movement. The dominant animal will force its subordinates to move, or conversely will at times inhibit their movement.

Flight is survival to the horse. When we control movement, we control flight. Control of movement leads to control of the horse's mind. It establishes leadership. Skilled trainers know that control of the horse's head and neck, lateral flexions and later vertical flexion, is essential for mastery of their mount. They also know that control of the feet leads to control of the entire horse.

I am teaching a foal to lead by following my hand which takes advantage of imprint training. Notice that its steps are synchronized with mine as it fearlessly leaves its mother.

Photo courtesy of Debby Miller.

Usually, in traditional training methods, the horse is taught to yield its head and neck after it is relatively mature. In traditional training methods, yielding of the feet and legs is mostly limited to allow hoof trimming.

However, when newborn foals are handled in the manner I advocate, the horses learn to yield their head, neck and feet before they ever stand or even nurse. They learn to do this quickly, before they have the physical strength to resist our manipulations, thereby learning that resistance is impossible. Most important, they never forget what they have learned shortly after birth because they are a precocial species in which the critical learning times occur during the immediate postpartum period.

Horse training consists largely of teaching horses to ignore harmless but frightening stimuli (desensitization) and also to respond to other stimuli (sensitization) until those responses become conditioned responses.

Both of the above can be taught easily, quickly, lastingly and safely and without trauma to the newborn foal. Many behaviors are, as yet, unprogrammed at that stage of life. Previous learning does not have to be re-programmed. For these reasons alone, what I call "imprint training" is preferable to any other system of training horses. There are two other major advantages to this method: bonding with humans and establishing dominance.

Bonding with Humans: First, because the training ideally begins as soon after birth as possible, it occurs during the imprinting period. The foal will automatically bond with the person or persons who are handling it just as it bonds with its dam. Remember that imprinting is a visual response. The foal born in the wild must bond not only with its dam, but also with the other members of its herd. Survival in a world filled with hungry predators depends to a great extent upon the foal's ability to keep up with the herd fleeing danger. Therefore, multiple imprinting is possible. The wolf cub must be imprinted not only by its mother, but also by its littermates and the other members of the pack. The duckling follows not only its mother, but also the siblings in front of it. Foals imprinted by humans regard our species with an accepting attitude that is discernibly different to the experienced observer, than do foals unexposed to human beings. That attitude is one of acceptance, recognition, free of fear, yet respectful.

Establishing Dominance Heirarchy: Throughout the foal procedure, within the first several days after birth, when we control the movement of the foal, it accepts our dominance. Our leadership role is automatically established and repeatedly reinforced. When we perform the post-partum desensitizing manipulations, the foal wants to get up and run away. It is thinking flight. We disallow that and, therefore, establish our dominance.

Conversely, in the sensitizing procedures we perform during the following days, we make the foal move.

We condition it to tactile signals to move in all directions, on command. Again, we are controlling movement and we reinforce our dominant role. A foal that is psychologically dependent upon us will, if mistakes aren't made later in training to betray it, become a horse which is very willing and highly responsive to performance training.

We should clarify what may seem to some readers to be a contradiction. We have stated that imprint training creates a foal that is free from fear of us. Yet, we have admitted, in our immediate post partum habituation procedure, to flooding the foal with frightening stimuli. There is no contradiction here. The newborn foal doesn't fear us. We are "mother." We imprint upon the foal. What does frighten the foal are the stimuli we flood it with: rubbing it with a plastic sheet, the noise of the clippers, tapping its hooves, rubbing its ears, the sight of a flapping blanket, the hissing sprayer and so on. This is why it is important to continue flooding until well after obvious habituation and relaxation occurs. We want that fearful, flighty response to harmless sensory stimuli to be extinguished forever.

Many people are concerned that handling the foal as soon as it is born, even before the mare bonds with it, may cause an interference with bonding and may predispose the mare to reject the foal. In forty years of experience with this method, I have never seen any evidence of bonding failure and, in fact, I have never seen the mare reject the foal. Rejection is a serious problem, sometimes due to a painful udder, but more often is due to a fear of the foal. This problem is most common in first foal Arabian mares which have led sheltered lives and have not seen many newborn foals. Imprint training, actually prevents rejection by such mares because they are encouraged by the trainer's presence and soon habituate to the foal the trainer is handling. Once they lick the foal out of curiosity, they are hooked. The maternal instinct kicks in.

There is no urgency for the foal to nurse during the first hour or two after foaling. However, studies at the University of California have shown that the administration of four to six ounces of colostrum, as soon as possible after foaling, (via baby bottle or syringe), will help to protect the foal against sepsis (infection). Septic foals are the most important cause of death in the newborn. Accordingly, I have made the feeding of the colostrum part of my training procedure for newborn foals.

Done correctly, the imprint-trained foal is calm, unafraid, friendly, respectful, responsive and willing to learn. Isn't that what we ideally seek to achieve in the domestic horse?

Chapter 13

Conditioned Responses

Horse training consists primarily of establishing conditioned responses. Conditioning is a process where the behavioral response becomes increasingly consistent as a result of reinforcement. Reinforcement occurs following the response to a stimulus. Reinforcement can be comfortable or uncomfortable to the subject ("reward" or "punishment"). The comfort or discomfort may be physical or psychological (emotional).

Physical comfort includes air, water, food, shelter, rest and grooming (stroking). Physical discomfort includes pain, work, extremes of temperature, or annoying stimuli such as prodding, tapping, or poking.

Psychological comfort includes praise, soothing sounds and pleasant sights. Psychological discomfort includes fear and reprimand. Psychological discomfort exists where there may be impending physical discomfort. Thus, a horse has fear (a psychological discomfort) because it is fearful of pain (a physical discomfort). Ultimately, all of the classifications we have created for reinforcement, such as "reward and punishment," "pleasure and pain," "fear and reassurance," can be simply classified as "comfort" and "discomfort." These are the reinforcing tools we use to condition responses in horses.

Classical (Respondent) Conditioning: *Classical conditioning* is illustrated by Pavlov's well-known technique of presenting two associated stimuli until one will cause a response similar to the other. Pavlov used food and a bell to create the conditioned response of salivation in dogs. Eventually, the sound of the bell alone would cause his dogs to salivate. Salivation was the conditioned response. If the food is omitted, then eventually the conditioned response will gradually become extinct. The dog will stop salivating at the sound of the bell.

Operant (Instrumental) Conditioning: *Operant conditioning* means that reinforcement is given only after the desired behavior is exhibited. For example, say we are teaching a horse to back up by pulling back on the reins. This creates discomfort for the horse. It tentatively takes a step back. We reward the horse by instantly releasing the pressure which provides comfort. The comfort is physical. We can provide additional physical comfort by sitting quietly for a full minute. Rest is an additional reward. Perhaps we stroke the horse briefly and say "Good boy!" Sooner or later this phrase will come to mean acceptance or praise by the horse. It is psychologically comforting.

Horses usually learn with three identical sensory experiences. Soon the horse will back one step when the rein is pulled back. After that response is conditioned, the other rewards (rest and praise) should be eliminated or they will be expected. After a single step back occurs in response to the tightened rein, a second step can be requested, with a pause between the steps. The number of steps back can be gradually increased while the interval between them is decreased. This process is called *Successive Approximation.* Ultimately the goal achieved will be a dramatic example of operant conditioning. The horse will trot backward in response to a very subtle signal - reining back.

Both classical conditioning and operant conditioning require reinforcement to become consistently and firmly established. The main difference between them is that classical conditioning is automatic and involuntary, whereas operant conditioning is deliberate and voluntary. In either case, the response eventually becomes habitual.

Both, however, are acquired gradually and one of the requirements of an effective trainer, therefore, is patience. Another is perceptivity, because the faster the reinforcement is provided (a concept known as *Immediacy*), the faster the behavior will become conditioned. The magnitude of the reinforcement is also a contributing factor to the speed of conditioning. The more intense the comfort or discomfort, the faster the behavior will be encouraged or discouraged.

A dramatic example of a conditioned response exists in the actions of a well-trained cutting horse. Although the cutting horse may make the most vivid example of operant conditioning in the art of horse training, the same principle exists in all other disciplines. Jumping horses, dressage horses, driving horses and even racehorses must be conditioned to respond to signals. Even the rodeo bucking horse becomes conditioned to its event. An old, experienced bucking horse is quiet in the chute while the rider mounts. Then, when the gate is opened, it responds to that stimulus, along with the pressures of the rigging or saddle and the flank strap by vigorous and enthusiastic bucking, usually stopping when the whistle or horn blows. Most of these horses develop a predictable style that is a behavior created by the reinforcing satisfaction of unseating many riders.

Unfortunately many conditioned responses develop in horses which are unwanted. Examples of undesirable conditioned behaviors in horses include pawing at feeding time, bucking or rearing, resisting girthing, moving off while being mounted, head shyness or ear shyness, "goosiness," rearing under saddle, running away, shying, bolting, bucking under saddle, kicking, pulling back and grazing while under way. These behaviors can be modified according to specific techniques that will be discussed later.

Chapter 14

Fixing and Improving
Conditioned Responses

Understanding that desired behavioral responses can be established in horses by reinforcing those responses, we can now examine the methods by which we can firmly fix or set those responses and enhance them to the highest possible degree.

In training horses, "rewards" are the most effective reinforcers because "punishment" elicits a flight response in this species and flight, as a rule, alienates the horse toward us.

Perhaps I should qualify this concept. Flight may be a desirable response in many cases. For example, we want a flight response in a racehorse, or in other speed events such as rodeo roping, barrel racing, etc. We also want a partial flight response in cutting horses, in dressage maneuvers, in jumping, in reining and so on. However, the flight reaction ideally should not be *from* us, but *with* us. The horse should see the rider as the herd leader to flee with, not as a predator to flee from. The reinforcing stimulus then, even if caused by the rider, should not be seen that way by the horse.

If rewards are the most effective reinforcers in conditioning behavioral responses in horses, let us next consider the kinds of rewards that are available to us.

As I stated earlier, I really prefer not to use the terms "reward" and "punishment" because they have connotations which may elicit a negative attitude in many people. Reward for example, may be interpreted as a bribe. Bribes are most effective in a reasoning species such as our own, but they are not especially effective in horses. Punishment on the other hand is suggestive of cruel, malicious or vengeful motivations on our part and these have absolutely no place in the training or handling of horses.

Therefore, I prefer to use the terms "comfort" and "discomfort," either of which can be physical or psychological. Fear is a psychological discomfort, yet it has physical origins. Fear, as an emotion in horses, is based upon what? It is fear of pain, a physical quality, or fear of death, a very physical state.

So, what sorts of comfort can we provide horses, to use as reinforcement for desirable behavior? Let's list the "comforts."

Air: A horse can only live a few minutes without air, so it can be used as a profound reward; a source of comfort. For example, according to the *Jeffery Method of Breaking Wild Horses*, the horse is confined to a small enclosure and the trainer has a noose around the horse's neck. Whenever the horse faces away from the trainer the noose is tightened which inhibits breathing. The instant the horse faces toward the trainer the noose is given slack and the horse can breathe more freely. Comfort! The horse soon learns to face the handler.

During a training workout at speed, the horse becomes winded. The respiratory rate is greatly increased in order to meet the oxygen demands of the body. Suddenly the horse does a particularly effective stop, turn or change of leads. The wise trainer immediately rewards the horse by allowing it to stop and rest. After several repetitions, the horse will associate the behavior with the opportunity to catch up with his respiratory needs and will try to repeat the performance on command.

As another example, let's say the horse is training in an area and one particular spot causes shying. This is a very common problem and is caused by the memory of a frightening stimulus, or by a stimulus to which the horse has become sensitized. Perhaps on a previous occasion the horse saw a cat or some other animal emerge or disappear in that area. Or perhaps there is a frightening flag, strange object, or an unfamiliar odor there. Many trainers physically force the horse to go to the problem area. This is what causes chronic shying. The horse is saying, "I'm afraid I'll get hurt," and with whip or spur we hurt the horse, thereby confirming that fear.

If, instead, we simply canter the horse for a long time in an area in which he feels safe, until he is winded and then stop and allow him to catch his breath near the shying point, it will become an area of comfort.

After several repetitions, each time stopping a little closer to the frightening spot, the horse will begin to seek it. What was the source of mental discomfort (fear) will become transformed into a source of physical comfort (air). Problem solved, without abuse and without making the horse afraid of us.

Water: A horse can live only a few days without water, so water is second only to air as a source of comfort. It can, therefore, be used as reinforcement for desirable behavior, *if* the horse is thirsty. A frightening area or place, such as an unfamiliar stall, or a trailer, can become a very desirable place for a thirsty horse to go into if it provides the only source of water. "Barn sour" and "herd bound" horses can be made to look forward to a ride away from home if they are thirsty and learn that they can drink when they get to where they are going. Horses in the wild only drink once or twice a day, so a domestic horse needs to be thirsty if water is to be used for reinforcing behavior.

Food: Horses are a species which, in nature, graze from 10 to 17 hours a day. A circus trainer client once told me when I asked how he was able to teach three dolphins to simultaneously, in formation, do a double flip out of the water, "Doc! Anything that eats can be trained!"

Most horse trainers rarely use food rewards, yet small palatable treats such as slices of carrot or apple can be extremely effective reinforcers in training horses or in simply changing their attitude toward us. The only horse trainers that I have seen use food rewards liberally are some circus trainers. Most notably, the Circus Knie, the national circus of Switzerland and arguably the best show of its kind in the world, is best known for its dazzling horse acts. Many horses used in their acts are stallions, often dozens of them performing simultaneously in a single small ring. They are frequently rewarded with tidbits. This is done in training and during the performances as well. The Knie family has used these techniques for generations. The classical riding schools in Europe liberally use food rewards to reinforce training.

Obviously, food is most effective if the horse is somewhat hungry, but actually this species is always hungry if the treat is highly palatable. Food treats used as reinforcement are most effective when offered as a single small tidbit. Slices of carrot are more effective than whole carrots. A pinch of grain is better than a pan full. Why? I don't know. Perhaps after the first bite the horse forgets why it was offered.

Immediacy is always an important concept in reinforcement. The reward should be offered as soon as possible after the desired behavior occurs. The reversed concept deserves mention here. A horse, returning to the stable after a ride or drive, should never be fed right away. To do so encourages the "barn sour" vice in which the horse jigs and constantly tries to hurry home. Don't we all like to hurry home to comfort, rest and a good meal?

Rest: Even when a horse is not winded rest can be used as reinforcement for desired behavior. As a rule, animals work because they must. Rest, therefore, is a welcome respite. Yet, there are exceptions to this statement. Certainly many of us work because we really enjoy it. A Border Collie loves to work livestock. It is genetically compelled to do so. Hounds love to hunt, retrievers love to retrieve, racehorses love to run and cats love to hunt. Still, rest can be a reward when we approve of a given behavior.

Affection: Creatures which live in groups in nature crave acceptance by their peers. That's why dogs are delighted when we reward behavior with approval manifested by stroking or saying "Good dog!" Conversely, they are made very uncomfortable if we express disapproval. Try that with a cat! Cats are loners and are much less reactive to either approval or disapproval by their owners. This doesn't mean that cats can't get along with other cats, or with other creatures, bond with them, or enjoy affection. It just means that they don't need us, as does a pack hunter like a dog that relies upon the alpha individual to lead it.

Horses aren't hunters, but they are herd animals and in the wild they are quite reliant upon a herd leader to protect them from danger. Horses, therefore, are reinforced in their behavior by praise and affection, if used promptly and briefly to reward that behavior. Moreover, horses are a mutually grooming species, so stroking or petting is a naturally agreeable action to them.

An expression such as "Good boy!" or "Good girl!" can be consistently linked with brief stroking to reward desired behavior and eventually the stroking can be phased out leaving the auditory expression as the sole reward. This increases the horse's comfort and horses crave comfort.

Security: In this species, the most timid and flighty of all domestic animals, a sense of security, psychological comfort or safety can become a profound source of reinforcement. A vivid example of this is the method used to teach a horse to load into a horse trailer when, due to previous experience, the horse has learned to fear the trailer.

The horse is first conditioned to move forward and backward on command, when not in the presence of the trailer. Once this response is completely conditioned, the horse is asked to go forward, toward the trailer, from a distance. The encouraging stimulus is some sort of intimidating but not painful, repetitious, uncomfortable action. It might be tapping with a stick or crop, or a whirling lead rope. Any movement towards the trailer, even a partial step, is immediately rewarded by comfort. The stimulus stops. The horse is petted and praised. It is then walked in a circle or backed a few steps on command. With patience and persistence this process is repeated until the horse realizes that comfort only lies in the direction of the trailer. Ultimately, it will tentatively touch one foot to the trailer. This effort merits extra praise and rest. When finally the horse puts both forefeet in the trailer, extraordinary praise should be given and the horse promptly backed out on command.

Soon, the horse will appreciate the trailer as a sanctuary from mental and physical discomfort. Still, the horse should not be locked in the trailer, even if he completely loads. Instead, back him out and begin the harassing stimuli again always stopping at any effort to get in the trailer.

The lesson isn't over until the horse loves the trailer. There is peace, security, rest and relaxation in the trailer. As soon as he is asked to back out trouble begins. He has to work and worry. The annoying stimulus begins again. It is better to be in the trailer. Horses crave security. The place they want to be is wherever they regard as a safe haven.

Unfortunately, many people attempting to teach horses to load teach the horse that the trailer is a place of unrest, pain, fear and excitement. No wonder so many horses refuse to load and no wonder trailer loading injuries are so commonly seen by veterinarians in equine practice.

Ideally, it is best to plan a trailer-loading lesson when you have time to complete the entire lesson from start to finish. When you are in a hurry to load up and get somewhere is not the time to "fix" a horse that won't load into the trailer. If you begin the lesson and give up before the horse is loading completely and sees the trailer as a place of security and comfort, the horse will learn that it doesn't always have to load when

81

asked. What is reinforced is that if the horse refuses enough, you will give up and the annoying stimulus will "go away." Again, patience and persistence (which take time) are the important aspects of any training lesson.

Chapter 15

Techniques for Enhancing
Conditioned Responses

Training horses may involve any of the behavior shaping and behavior modifying techniques described previously such as habituation, or domination via flight control. Most trained behaviors in domestic horses, however, are conditioned responses. The visual, auditory and tactile stimuli, which we use to elicit a learned response, are the signals which lead to the desired behaviors necessary for horses to perform in their specific disciplines. Horses change leads, circle barrels, do intricate dressage maneuvers, spin and slide in reining classes, do the ballet of the cutting horse and jump the formidable obstacles on a cross country course because they have been conditioned to do so.

It has been shown that newborn foals can be conditioned to respond as quickly or even more quickly than older horses. Subsequent training sessions, if compatible with those done initially, will further refine and improve the conditioned responses. Regardless of the age of the horse when the initial conditioned responses are established, progressive improvement in those responses depends upon the use of appropriate reinforcing techniques. The kinds of reinforcement most effective for horses include air, water, food, rest, stroking and praise. The means by which these positive reinforcements are applied is critical in order to obtain the best results.

The awkward turning of the green colt can be transformed into the whirling spin of the finished reining horse only by a competent and knowledgeable trainer. The same can be said of the bouncing, halting stop of the green colt compared to the smooth sliding stop later on. The awkward half pass of a novice dressage horse can be compared to the graceful movements of the higher level horse, or the early jumps of a future cross-country prospect can be compared to the spectacular leaps of the seasoned competitor.

Refining and improving conditioned responses, even when appropriate reinforcing measures are applied, requires certain methods of applying those measures.

Immediacy: The more closely the "reward" follows the behavior, the more quickly the behavior will become fixed. It requires human reasoning ability for a reward to be effective long after the behavior is elicited. For example: "If you'll help do the dishes this week, I'll take you to the zoo next weekend." Or - "If you can increase your sales by ten percent, you will get a raise in salary." Horses cannot be expected to respond to such delayed reinforcement. Immediate comfort or immediate relief from discomfort works for horses. Sometimes referred to as the "Three Second Rule," the reward must be offered within three seconds of the desired behavior or the horse will not be able to establish a connection between the reward and the behavior.

The slightest effort should be profoundly rewarded. It appeals to human reason to say "You made a 70 on your last test. That's not bad, but I think you can do better. If you'll make an 80 on the next test, I'll buy you those roller skates." For horses, the reward must come for any improved performance. Indeed, the most perceptive and skilled trainers seem to reward the horse's *thought* of improved performance. If, for example, the horse is being taught to back, then leaning back, or even the faintest movement of one leg backwards or even a shift in weight should be rewarded by an immediate release from pressure. Comfort! Gradually, this movement can be transformed into backing with quickness and rhythmic grace by means of Successive Approximation.

Successive Approximation: The dramatic slides and spins of the Western reining horse, the incredible dodging movements of a finished cutting horse, or the perfectly executed and collected movements of a high level dressage horse are produced tediously, gradually and progressively by Successive Approximation. The horse learns in small, improving increments - each step being reinforced positively with some sort of reward, however small. Continuing with the example of backing, the horse learns to get relief from pressure by yielding backward one step. Later, the

84

trainer asks for a second step and then a third, each with a pause (a rest) in between. The horse is receiving two rewards: a relief from pressure, which is a discomfort, and a brief rest, which is a comfort. Eventually these small steps are linked into what is literally a trot backwards. Exceptional efforts can be rewarded with praise, stroking, or an extra "vacation" by dismounting for a while.

Additionally, other signals can be used simultaneously or just prior to the pressure of the rein. The word "back" can be used, for example. Or, a change in seat position is a practical bridging signal because it is an advantage to the rider's balance in rapid backing. Ultimately, a transition can be made to the verbal signal, or the change in seat position to get the horse to back, using the rein with subtly, or not at all, saving it in case there is an inadequate response to the bridging signal.

Consistency: The greatest obligation required of an effective horse trainer is consistency. Until a behavior is firmly fixed as a conditioned behavioral response, the trainer must be consistent in applying signals and in granting rewards. Nothing confuses a horse more than inconsistency. This is why the best results are obtained if only one trainer uses the horse, especially when it is first learning. Later on, with experience, horses can learn to perform dependably even with varied and sometimes inept handlers. Many ranches have older cow horses that can do their job despite being ridden by different riders, many of whom are not skilled horsemen. On the other hand, horses at a stable that are constantly ridden by numerous incompetent people cannot be expected to perform well.

Imagine how confused the horse must be whose rider says, "whoa" repeatedly when the horse fidgets, or when a slower gait is desired. How is the horse supposed to know that "whoa" means to stop - and nothing else? Other commands must be used to control fidgeting or to obtain a slower gait.

If the spurs are used to move a horse laterally and also to request forward movement, how is the horse supposed to know in which direction to go when spurred? How many riders understand that lateral control of the hindquarters is obtained by the use of the rider's legs? In fact, how many riders appreciate that all movement by the horse, in any direction, originates in the hinduarters? How many riders understand that forward movement of the horse comes from creating pressure behind the horse? If all riders understood that we would not see horses being whipped on the neck or forequarters in order to encourage forward movement.

If we ask a horse to do something and he responds improperly and is physically abused by us for doing so, the horse thinks that *trying* to respond is a crime. On the other hand, if the horse responds correctly but inadequately and is physically abused, he will again think that trying is a crime. Consistently rewarding effort encourages horses to do better next time. Reinforce the slightest response.

Variable Rewards: Once a behavior is consistently elicited as a conditioned response, it can be enhanced by means of a variable reward schedule. For example, let's consider teaching horses to be caught. This is best done in a confined area, haltering the horse, briefly stroking him, giving him a small food reward (after he is haltered) and then turning him loose. As soon as the horse realizes that haltering is rewarded with affection, a food reward and then being turned loose, he will soon be glad to be haltered. A word command like "come" can be used as a bridging stimulus. Eventually, most horses will not only respond to "come," but will stick their noses into the halter knowing that a food reward will promptly follow.

Once that behavior is consistently and invariably exhibited - conditioned - then a variable reward schedule may be instituted which, curiously, will enhance the response even further. The desired behavior is now rewarded unpredictably. Perhaps with food and affection this time, perhaps with either next time, perhaps with just a "good boy!" the time after that. A variable reward schedule improves the response. When, occasionally, the horse is actually put to work, it is probably a good idea to see that a particularly desirable reward precedes the work. Do not be surprised if the horse learns to anticipate which time it will be turned loose, or perhaps just groomed, just tied for a while or actually put to work. Remember how perceptive these animals are. They will learn to observe which boots you are wearing, which halter you are carrying, or whether you have the tack room door unlocked prior to saddling.

The slot machines in Las Vegas are programmed with a variable reward schedule designed to keep the player at the machine, investing coins for an occasional reward in an ultimately and necessarily losing game.

Generalization of Behavior: It is important to understand that once a trained behavior is fully conditioned in a given location, it is necessary to obtain the same results in multiple locations in order for the behavior to become generalized.

It is possible, due to our power to reason, to train a human in a single location and then convey the idea that the same behavior is to be expected in any location, but animals cannot understand that concept. This is the reason that some people take their dog to an obedience class, get satisfactory results and then become dismayed at their pet's performance at home or elsewhere.

Similarly, it is common for horses to perform impressively at the home stable and then fall apart at a show or other location. Horses require the same lesson at three or more locations before they begin to understand that the same behavior is expected everywhere. Four, five, six or more locations generalize the behavior even more. When showhorse trainers take green horses to a show to "season" them, what they hope to do is to desensitize the horse to alarming stimuli and to generalize trained responses. In training, it is wise to elicit the same conditioned responses in as many different locations as possible.

When a horse is well trained at the home stable and becomes unmanageable at a strange location, it emphasizes the importance of communicating with horses by achieving a dominant leader's role, rather than by using fear.

Chapter 16

Counter-Conditioning

Horses frequently develop unwanted behavior. That is, the behavior in question is unwanted by us. To the horse the behavior may be acceptable, or even satisfying. Unwanted behaviors often become conditioned responses because some kind of reinforcement occurs as a result of the behavior. The reinforcement may be positive or negative, but if it in any way makes the horse more comfortable, the behavior is more likely to be repeated until it becomes a habitual conditioned response. Remember that with horses, as with dogs or children, a negative response, such as punishment, is sometimes rewarding in that it gains attention.

Much misbehavior is simply an attempt to gain attention, which is why punishment often makes misbehavior worse. Punishment (discomfort) is best used in such a manner that the subject assumes that it is punishing itself rather than blaming us for it. As an example, I discourage baby foals from touching my hands or body with their mouths by flicking a finger sharply at their muzzle. When I do this I look away from the foal and use no hand or arm movement that the foal will learn to associate with the misbehavior. Instead I just flick the muzzle as it touches me. The effect I want is as if touching me results in an electric shock. The effect, if my timing and consistency are good, is to extinguish the foal's desire to nuzzle me or nibble at me, which is an unwanted behavior in the mature horse.

Because horses learn so quickly, conditioned misbehaviors take a variety of forms and have been traditionally called "vices." These vices have been classified as "vices under saddle," or "stable vices."

Stable vices or vices on the ground include kicking, crowding, cribbing or windsucking, pulling back when tied, rushing backwards out of a stall or trailer, tearing blankets, weaving, head shyness, chewing wood, stall walking, pawing or digging, restlessness when being saddled or mounted and refusing to be lead.

Vices under saddle include rearing, bolting, running away, "barn sour" (refusing to leave the stable), jibbing or jogging, bucking, shying, kicking, biting, boring (overflexing the head and neck while in the bit) and "herd bound" (refusing to leave the company of a companion horse).

Most of these vices can become conditioned responses when the horse perceives the reinforcement as a desirable thing and the rewarding comfort may not be obvious to us. For example, the punishment may gain the horse some desired attention. In the case of some annoying vices such as cribbing, there may be a physiological reward. Cribbing is a repetitive form of seemingly purposeless behavior. Cribbing is harmful to the horse because it causes excessive dental wear. Many horse owners confuse cribbing with wood chewing. Cribbing is properly defined as a habit in which the horse bites on any edge (usually the preferred edge is wood), stiffens the muscles of the throat and emits a grunt. Wind sucking has traditionally and erroneously been believed to involve the actual swallowing of air, which leads to chronic flatulence. These types of behavior are known as "stereotypic behaviors" or "stereotypies."

Research at Tufts University reveals that such behaviors, usually a reaction to some sort of stress, cause the brain to produce narcotic-like substances, the endorphins. It is addiction to these endorphins, produced by the individual's own body, that perpetuates the stereotypical behavior. The stress that is most commonly associated with the onset of cribbing in horses is isolation. Horses, of all animals, are a grazing, flighty prey species that need a lot of room to roam and lots of company. Experiments using narcotic antagonist drugs, which neutralize the endorphins, have caused temporary cessation of the stereotypical behavior. This tends to substantiate the theory that chronic stereotypies are indeed the result of endorphin addiction.

Confinement to a stall, or other limited enclosure, is psychologically stressful, especially to young and inexperienced horses. Stereotypical behaviors that cause endorphin elaboration are expected consequences of confinement and isolation. Horses need company. Similar stereotypies are common in other confined animals. Examples include feather plucking in caged birds, "hot spots" and acral (lick) dermatitis in bored dogs, tail sucking in cats and cage walking in closely confined zoo animals. Horses, being a flight species, are understandably the most frequent victims and some of the stereotypical behaviors seen are self-mutilating or destructive. Biting at the horse's own skin is an example, as is excessive water consumption (polydipsia nervosa), eating sand or other unwholesome substances (pica) and stall kicking to the point where serious leg trauma results.

Some young horses, even if not stressed physically or mentally, may develop stereotypical behaviors by imitating that behavior when it is seen in another horse. This imitative behavior is called *allelomimetic behavior*. It occurs in many species and I'll say more about it later because it can be used to create desirable behavior as well as undesirable. Young stock is best kept away from confirmed cribbers or horses with other behavior faults, although recent research questions the long-held opinion that young horses can learn cribbing from older addicts.

There are several ways to cope with unwanted behavior patterns in horses.

Ignore the behavior. This is often the best strategy, especially if the behavior is not yet a conditioned response. Ignoring it, at least initially, at least serves to avoid reinforcing it negatively.

Condition an incompatible behavior. This is a technique frequently used by trainers to cope with vices under saddle such as shying, jigging, boring, etc. The rider will turn the horse whenever the unwanted behavior occurs, disengaging the hindquarters and making tight circles. This often serves to gradually discourage the unwanted behavior, but skill and alertness are required of the rider. In other words, it takes a good horseman to do this effectively.

Punish the unwanted behavior as soon as it occurs. As said earlier, this is ideally done so that the horse assumes that it is punishing itself. If we can create in the horse's mind the idea that we are a sanctuary from punishment (even though we are doing it), then we are able to not only extinguish the unwanted behavior without alienating the relationship with the horse, but we can actually enhance that relationship.

To eliminate an unwanted behavior, we counter-condition by causing a distracting, uncomfortable stimulus every time the behavior occurs. If done correctly, the speed with which this can be effective is somewhat startling.

Here's an example of how to apply counter-conditioning for a common problem such as "hard to catch." Many horses are hard to catch, that is, they do not willingly stand to be haltered or run away when a person approaches. The owner usually begins the process by approaching the horse while hiding the halter behind the back (as if this most perceptive of all animals doesn't know!) then some treat such as grain is used to persuade the horse to allow the owner to "catch" it. The owner doesn't realize that when feed is used to catch a horse it is the owner who is being trained.

A simple but effective method to change this behavior is to use counter-conditioning. The horse should be in a relatively small confined area. A round pen, 50 or 60 feet in diameter is ideal, but one a bit smaller or twice that size will do.

As we approach the horse quietly, in a non-threatening way, it will move away from us. We immediately "punish" this behavior by frightening the horse. This can be done by aggressively waving a flag at it made of a stick or dressage whip with a piece of noisy white plastic secured to one end. Or, we can flip a length of rope at the horse. What I do is affect a hunched over predatory stance (I learned this from watching Border Collies herd sheep and like those wonderful dogs, I accompany this predatory stance with an intimidating stare.) Whichever method is used, this precipitates flight in the horse, increasing its attempts to escape us.

The horse's eyes and ears will be directed out of the pen, its nose pointed outward and its body arched away from us. These body positions indicate its desire to escape us and as long as they persist, our pursuit should continue to create further mental discomfort. Eventually, however, when the horse realizes that escape is impossible, it will look at us. This point may be fleeting but is discernible when the ear closest to you points toward you. At that instant the horse is looking at you. Instantly assume a passive stance and look down or away from the horse. If you are using a flag or rope, let it passively drop to the ground. Then, the moment the ear points away from you, resume the pursuit.

If your responses are immediate and exaggerated (very aggressive or conversely, very passive) the horse will learn after several repetitions that it is safest when it looks at you. It will soon stop and face you. At that point, increase its comfort by passively backing away from the horse, avoiding eye contact. Within a few minutes the formerly hard-to-catch horse will be walking towards you. Any time it looks or moves away from you, pursue it. Whenever it looks or moves toward you, reward it by becoming passive and moving away. You can not only catch a horse with this technique, quickly extinguishing its habit of running away, but you can actually persist in this procedure until the horse will follow you wherever you go.

Each time you catch the horse, reward it with praise and a few strokes and then release it. Once the horse's behavior changes, it is important to repeat the lesson in several different locations in order to generalize the response.

This counter-conditioning can be reinforced every time you go out to the pasture to catch a horse with the halter and lead rope in your hand. If the horse moves away from you, swing the end of the lead rope at the horse to cause it to move even more. Don't "chase" the horse; just cause it to move away from you. When the horse looks at you, assume a passive stance with your head down and body turned slightly away from the horse (keep the horse in sight from the corner of your eye). When the horse stops, it may come to you, but if not, approach again in a very passive manner. If the horse moves away, make it move again. Repeat these steps until the horse either comes to you or stands still when you approach. The horse will eventually learn that it is much less work (more comfortable) to stand still and be caught than running away each time you approach with a halter.

Although a conditioned response, such as moving away when approached with a halter, can be quickly extinguished by this counter-conditioning technique, it will at first be effective only in that specific location. The lesson must be repeated in multiple locations before the behavior is consistently altered in any possible location.

Counter-conditioning techniques to deal with another common problem, the head-shy horse, are demonstrated in two video tapes which I have made: *Influencing the Horse's Mind,* and *Control of the Horse.*

Counter-conditioning can be used to alter many other kinds of undesirable conditioned responses. Many horses have habits that are unpleasant under saddle. On a trail ride, the horse that jigs and becomes impatient on the way home is an example. If, every time this occurs, discomfort is caused by disengaging the hindquarters and making the horse turn several times, eventually an association will be made between cause and effect and the behavior will change. The rider, of course, must be very patient, very persistent and absolutely consistent in order for this to work. Not all riders are endowed with these qualities.

Chapter 17

Claustrophobia

Remember when you were a child and loved to play in boxes, tents and playhouses? Even people who later in life become claustrophobic and fear enclosed places like closets or elevators enjoyed small shelters as a child. Forts, caves, tents and tree houses are a part of growing up. Children love to snuggle under the bedclothes especially when they are frightened or feel insecure. What child has not delighted in crawling into a packing box or shipping carton? Like many other species, we are a denning species.

We are a predatory species. We're cave dwellers, biologically speaking. It's no surprise that we instinctively enjoy enclosed spaces unless some trauma has taught us to fear them. Most of us are familiar with the feeling of comfort we so often gain when we enter our own automobile or pickup truck. It is familiar, secure territory. Our turf!

Similar behavior can be seen in other predatory species. Dogs and cats are hunters. Observe how kittens and pups love to crawl into sacks and enclosed spaces. They're cave dwellers, too. Coyotes are born in dens. So are cougars, bobcats and bears.

Horses are different. Horses are a prey species that evolved in an open grassland habitat. The natural enemies of the horse are the cave dwelling members of the cat and dog family - wolves and the giant cats.

The horse's primary defense is flight. Horses survive in the wild by sprinting away from perceived danger. Horses are, therefore, naturally claustrophobic. They instinctively fear enclosed spaces, or confinement of any kind. We humans are the opposite of horses in that respect. Confinement may mean safety and comfort to us. To a horse it could mean death.

Understanding the horse's natural claustrophobia helps us to sympathize with its reluctance to go through narrow, enclosed places, into unfamiliar stalls, through chutes and into horse trailers. It explains the panic of an unbroken colt if it is abruptly lassoed, hobbled, or saddled. It explains the horse's bucking when saddled for the first time. It is not so much the saddle that causes the bucking as the pressure of the cinch or girth that elicits a claustrophobic reaction. Most trainers, in starting a colt, will desensitize the back to the weight of the saddle, yet few of them desensitize the girth area (with repetitious rhythmic pressure). Accordingly, the colt bucks when first saddled, usually as soon as the cinch is tightened. If the girth area is adequately desensitized, most colts will not buck when initially saddled, although some of them will. Never assume an adult horse will accept a cinch or girth. This is a behavior that the horse must be conditioned to accept. Many horses that have not been properly conditioned to accept a cinch or girth are commonly labeled "cinchy" or "cinch shy." When cinching a horse, it is important to do so gradually. If a cinch or girth is pulled tightly in one aggressive tug, the horse may respond in a panic or flight response. Nowadays, most colt starters will allow the horse to become desensitized to the saddle and girth at liberty, before mounting. Good idea!

The claustrophobic reaction is what causes so many horses to injure themselves severely when caught in a wire fence. They panic, try to run and get cut. Mules are less likely to react in this way, not so much because they are smarter than horses, but because they are half donkey and donkeys are not as flighty as horses. Why? Because in the wild donkeys are mountain dwellers and blind flight could be disastrous to a mountain animal. Donkeys and their hybrid offspring mules are less claustrophobic than horses.

The accentuated bucking of rodeo broncs is due to the flank strap that compounds the claustrophobic stimulus of the saddle cinch. The flank strap does not cause bucking due to pain as is so often charged by anti-rodeo activists. In fact, a tight flank strap will immobilize a horse or bovine, a technique we veterinarians often use to restrain our patients for doctoring. A snug, but not tight, flank strap simply stimulates higher bucking action. Older, experienced bucking stock eventually buck as a learned behavioral response. Many of them seem to enjoy it just as performance horses can enjoy their particular event. But bucking begins as a claustrophobic reaction to confinement. Horses are claustrophobic.

Why then are we able to teach horses to work in harness, to ride into a herd of closely packed cattle, or into a Manhattan traffic gridlock, into trailers and palpating chutes, into tie stalls and all kinds of confining situations?

It is because this remarkable species can be so quickly desensitized to fear-provoking situations, if they are not hurt. Horses are remarkably adaptable. They are naturally flighty creatures, but the flight response can be quickly extinguished, so long as they are not hurt. Flighty animals must quickly desensitize to frightening but harmless stimuli or they would always be running. Thus, with correct training techniques, horses can be taught to overcome the claustrophobia of confinement. Moreover, once horses accept the confinement of a saddle, hobbles, a stake rope, a stall, or anything else that inhibits escape, they develop a more subordinate attitude. This means that they are more accepting of leadership, more reliant upon human guidance and more willing to work together with us.

Chapter 18

Copycat (Allelomimetic) Behavior

Imitative or copycat behavior (*allelomimetic behavior*) can occur in any species and at any stage of life, but it most profoundly influences the behavior of the very young. Parents, take heed! Horse breeders, beware!

Before discussing the significance of allelomimetic behavior in the horse, we should consider its presence in other species in order to appreciate its prevalence and appreciate the powerful influence it has on behavior.

Some quiet evening, when your dog is in repose, try sitting up alertly and with alarm in your voice, say, "What's that? Who's there?" Most dogs, even though they have sensed nothing suspicious, will mimic your attitude because you are (hopefully) your dog's surrogate pack leader and become acutely alert and territorially protective.

Most of us have seen motion pictures showing how lions and other big cats teach their cubs to hunt. They demonstrate the technique allowing the young to playfully accompany and mimic them, which conveys hunting skills and confidence to the cubs.

Ducklings, imprinted to follow their mother, duplicate her entry into water and thereby learn to swim. Allelomimetic behavior is involved in cattle stampedes and in human mobs stampeding at a soccer game or a concert.

When I was a boy, fist fighting was a daily occurrence in the schoolyard. The rules were learned in the movie theaters and strongly shaped our values and actions in those days. Hitting below the belt was a dastardly tactic and kicking or using a club or stone was considered cowardly. The use of a knife or gun was unthinkable.

It is interesting to watch small boys scuffle today, whether in play or in earnest. They whirl and kick, using martial arts moves they may have learned in a class, but are more likely to have learned from watching TV.

Previously, we mentioned how common it is for a young horse to pick up bad habits as a result of watching an older horse.

One reason many horses, especially green horses, get excited and want to run off if another horse runs past them is because of allelomimetic behavior. Conversely, putting a green draft horse in harness alongside a calm, steady, well-trained horse tends to calm the youngster. A common courtesy while trail riding is to announce your intention to your riding companions that you are going to change your horse's gait from a walk to a trot, for example. They can be prepared to either change with you or hold their horses back because the horses will want to instinctively move with the other horses.

It is interesting to note how, in halter classes at gaited horse shows, the person leading the horse moves like his or her charge with animation and impulsion. It encourages the horse to similar efforts.

In 1988, I was privileged to attend the national horse show in Lima, Peru. The show is limited to the Peruvian Paso, an extremely smooth moving, laterally gaited breed. The trainers, leading their horses in halter classes, move in a way to inspire their horses. Knees slightly flexed, upper bodies erect and motionless, they rapidly circle the ring in a gliding gait to mimic and encourage the horses they lead.

All foals tend to mimic the gait and stride cadence of their dams, especially when moving rapidly or when alarmed. This tendency is put to good use on the racetrack, or in driving teams.

The susceptibility of foals to emulate the behavior of their mothers or of other stablemates emphasizes the importance of having well-mannered broodmares. It is tragic that so many breeders neglect the training of mares. The mare, more than any other factor, will determine the temperament of the foal, both genetically and allelomimetically. Beyond that, it is up to us.

I feel so strongly about this that I recommend that an ill-mannered mare not be bred. Unless she is inherently evil, it only takes a few hours of work using methods described elsewhere, to teach a mare to be calm and respectful. This should always be done before she is ever bred.

The propensity of horses to mimic and especially to mimic gaits can be a useful tool to the trainer or handler. It can be used to solve certain behavioral quirks. For example, balking. Young horses hesitate because of fear and insecurity and unless the problem is handled properly, this kind of behavior can become habitual. I am a mule breeder and owner and mules, even more than horses, are known for their balkiness.

When a horse (or mule) being led balks, what most people do is turn to face the horse. The animal is balking because of some perceived threat. Direct eye contact from the handler is also perceived as a threat. Now, facing the person leading it, the horse is asked to invade their personal space. This only increases its intimidation, making the horse even more reluctant to move forward.

Often, the handler swings the lead rope, striking the horse behind. The horse is balking because it is afraid of being hurt. So, what do we do? We hurt it, thereby confirming its apprehension. Is it any wonder that many horses habitually balk and shy? Shying is simply the next step after balking - to turn and run from the perceived danger.

When a horse being led balks, it is far better to use allelomimetic behavior to overcome the problem. Perform the behavior you want your horse to imitate as follows: Do not look back at the horse. Instead, look forward, focus your gaze forward, elevate your chin and march in place with high knee action. It may take a while, but eventually the horse will be reassured. You seem to be moving forward and nothing has happened to you, so the horse will move forward. Sometimes after a step or two, it will balk again. Don't look back, just keep marching in place with a determinedly forward gaze. It may look silly, but it works and ultimately the horse will learn to trust your judgment and will be willing to follow you. It is significant how often the colt will synchronize its gait with yours when this technique is used.

Because foals will so often instinctively mimic the gait of the mare, step for step, I recommend leading the foal from the mare under saddle soon after it has learned to lead well from the ground. This should be done from both sides so that the foal doesn't become one-sided and should be done at a walk until the foal consistently leads alongside the mare without pulling back or rushing forward. Then the gait can be increased to a slow trot. Eventually the foal should move alongside the mounted mare at an extended trot and finally at a canter.

If for some reason the mare cannot be ridden, then the above procedure can be delayed until after the foal is weaned. Then it can be led from a gentle, well-trained horse in the same manner. Similarly, the foal, taught to tie, can be tied near the mare for longer periods of time learning to be patient and accepting.

Allelomimetic behavior can also serve as an asset when teaching foals to load into a horse trailer. If the mare loads quietly and cooperatively and is content in the trailer it is much easier to teach the foal to accept the trailer in the same manner.

Running alongside of her dam, the foal mimics the mare's gait step for step.
Photo courtesy of Tim Hannan Photography.[C]

Chapter 19

The Opposition Reflex

The tendency of an organism to move into pressure is called *Opposition Reflex (Positive Thigmotaxis)*. It is important to understand this reaction if we are to appreciate the behavioral reactions of animals to certain stimuli. The first time a leash and collar is used to lead a pup, a common reaction is for the pup to pull against the collar and choke itself. Our human reaction is to think; "You dummy! Stop resisting and you'll be more comfortable." It takes a long time for the dog to learn this and some dogs never seem to learn. This reaction to move into the pressure rather than yielding to it is an instinctive response.

Another example is vivid to me because I hand milked a lot of cows when I was young. When the cow steps on your toe and stands on it, it is very painful. We respond by pushing the cow in the opposite direction with our hand, or whatever happens to be handy. Invariably, before she finally moves over, the cow will move toward the pressure, greatly increasing the pain suffered by the unfortunate milker. I finally learned to wear steel-toed shoes that allowed me to laugh triumphantly as I pushed the cow away from me.

When training horses to lead or to rein the usual first response to the pressure is resistance due to opposition reflex. The skilled trainer maintains the pressure, which is uncomfortable for the horse, until it finally yields to the pressure. The trainer instantly releases it. Horses learn very quickly to seek comfort by yielding to pressure instead of reflexively opposing it. The good trainer then patiently fixes that response by repetition until the horse is conditioned to automatically yield. A sequence of such yields is progressively developed into a freely leading or freely reining horse.

103

Understanding opposition reflex and how to cope with it is essential for properly training horses. It is especially important when teaching them to stand tied.

One of the most common, vilest and most destructive habits that horses learn is to pull back when tied. It is responsible for many injuries and deaths in horses as well as damage to equipment. When lead ropes or halters break (or more commonly nowadays, when the halter buckles or lead shank snaps give way) the horse is often violently flipped over backwards. Fractured skulls, neck, withers or back are common. Sometimes they bruise or fracture the tail head or adjacent pelvic bones. People in back of such "pull back" or "fly back" horses may get run over. If the equipment fails to break, the horse may lose its footing. The object it's tied to may pull loose causing a catastrophic runaway. Or, the horse may ultimately rebound forward injuring itself or some person in front of it.

A common consequence not recognized by most horsemen is injury to the neck, especially if the horse is tied lower than its head height. Sprains to the vertebral ligaments, corresponding to human "whiplash" injuries, produce lamenesses that are difficult to diagnose, especially when cervical nerves are injured. Rupture of a ligament in the neck (pulled-down neck) is common. The pain and fear that result from such incidents often result in habitual pulling back. This further damages the horse, equipment and the owner's compassion.

When a young horse pulls back and is tied to an immovable object with unbreakable equipment the horse instantly panics. This is, after all, a creature whose salvation in the wild is flight. The initial pulling back, which is a flight response, is violently magnified by fear and pain. All of this can be prevented by *not* tying horses to immovable objects. If young horses are tied to elastic, which stretches and yields, yet does not allow complete escape, the opposition reflex is not precipitated. I use truck tire inner tubes, attached to a high, safe fence post or tree. When a horse pulls back, it simply stretches. The harder they pull, the more it stretches. When they eventually relax, the elastic snaps them forward and causes an uncomfortable experience. They punish themselves. The violent opposition reflex does not occur. The horse learns to stand patiently while tied. The horse does not experience pain or injury from this lesson, so it doesn't fear being tied. But it has learned that pulling back is fruitless and uncomfortable.

Nowadays, elastic tie ropes are commercially available. I still use inner tubes around the stable, but the elastic tie ropes are nice because they can actually be carried on a trail ride.

When training a young horse to tie in this manner, I don't initially tie the rope to the inner tube. I just loop it through and stand by, holding the end of the rope, in case of an intense reaction. I don't tie the horse until I see that it is conditioned to move forward anytime the lead rope is taut.

Foals as young as one day of age can be taught to tie this way, but instead of using elastic, I simply hold the lead rope in my hands. My body becomes a fence post and my arms become the elastic. If the foal

This foal is only 26 hours old and being taught to yield to halter pressure. My arms act like a fence post yet give when the foal pulls back. *Photo courtesy of Debby Miller*

starts to pull back, I yield my arms, going with it which aborts the opposition reflex. I gently increase the pressure until, finally, the foal moves forward. However slight that forward movement is, it is immediately rewarded by complete release of pressure. Comfort! After three such experiences, most foals are conditioned to move forward when

Soon the foal will yield to the pressure and move forward when it feels pressure. This response will be permanently fixed.

Photo courtesy of Debby Miller.

they feel the halter pressure (which, remember, is largely to the back of the neck). We have averted the effects of opposition reflex and taught the foal to stand tied and to move forward in response to halter pressure rather than launching itself backward.

Never assume an adult horse will stand when tied. This is a behavior that must be conditioned and not all horses have been conditioned to respond properly. Many people just assume that because a horse is an adult or mature, the horse will stand tied or will stand in crossties properly. Test the horse's ability to stand tied by using the same technique described above for teaching the young horse to tie. Take the test one step further by walking away from the horse when the rope is looped through an inner tube or moveable object. Some horses respond with panic at the thought of being left alone and will pull back to return to the herd. If the horse has not been taught to yield to the halter pressure, it will continue to pull back and do whatever it takes to flee.

Perhaps one more example of the effects of opposition reflex in the horse is appropriate here. Some horses, when backed out of a horse trailer, do so in great haste. Rushing out this way can be injurious to the horse, or to any person in back of the trailer. Horses can and should be taught to stand patiently, unrestrained, in a trailer until commanded to back out and when they do back out they should do so quietly. However, prevention is always easier than a cure and in fact, many horses that load and haul nicely, will rush out when unloaded.

One method of slowing them down is to push strongly against their chest or shoulder while unloading. Obviously, this should be done by inserting an arm through an opening in front of the horse and not by climbing into the trailer with it. Pushing the horse backwards will frequently slow the horse's unloading. Why? Because it causes the horse to resist being moved backward due to opposition reflex. Some horses, however, conditioned to move backward in response to chest or shoulder pressure, will not slow down.

Back in the days when draft horses were commonly kept in tie stalls (I'm afraid that I remember those days), it was not uncommon for a horse to crowd a person entering the stall against the side. Our usual response was to push back and when this often resulted in the horse increasing pressure towards us, our interpretation was usually that the horse was behaving maliciously. In fact, the response was usually due to opposition reflex. The problem is simple to prevent. The horse just needs to be conditioned to step away from us by tapping him with a stick or riding crop and rewarding him when he does so by stopping the tapping. A bridging stimulus may be used immediately beforehand by saying, "Get over," and eventually the horse will respond to this stimulus alone.

All of the preceding explains why horses respond best to intermittent stimuli such as rhythmic tugs on the rein or lead rope, tapping with a crop or dressage whip, or intermittent leg pressure rather than steady severe pressure which simply elicits an opposing pressure or opposition reflex.

107

Chapter 20

Problem Solving

During the question and answer sessions which conclude the seminars on equine behavior that I have conducted all over the world, certain problems are invariably presented. Because these problems are so common and universal, an examination of their cause, their prevention and their correction is warranted.

Here is a list of the four most common problems of equine misbehavior and how to apply non-coercive techniques to correct them:

1. Shying: Virtually all young horses shy (shying is also known as "spooking"). It is natural for horses to shy. Remember that the horse's primary defense is flight. Remember how extremely perceptive horses are. Understand how keen their senses are. Keep in mind that this animal has the fastest reaction time. That's why shying so often unseats riders, or at least can occur before the rider can react in time to avert the behavior. In theory, because horses are so easy to desensitize to frightening stimuli, shying should be an easy habit to prevent. Why then is this such a common vice and why does it persist in so many horses throughout their lifetime? It is because the conventional wisdom, taught by a majority of riding instructors, is wrong.

The young horse, shying at a frightening stimulus, something seen or perhaps heard, is usually subjected to the whip and the spur. "Make him face it!" mentors demand. "Force him up to it so he can see that it is harmless!" we are counseled. "Don't let him get away with that!" we are advised.

When a horse shys, what is he saying? He says, "I see something suspicious! I'm afraid that it will hurt me!"

So, what do we do? We hurt the horse! This doesn't discourage future shying. It confirms his fear. It reinforces the desire to flee. Shying in young horses can be overcome. This is the method I use:

I simply stop and allow the colt to study the frightening thing. I wait until it habituates to it. This point is determined by the colt's relaxation. Its ears and eyes are no longer focused at the point of alarm. Its tenseness disappears. Its head lowers. It sighs. The colt looks away from the frightening source.

I now ask the colt to step closer to the source of fear. If it still exhibits the desire to flee, I stop and allow it to look at the object again. This process is continued, regardless of how long it takes until the colt is close enough to the spot to actually contact it. If this can be done, it is rewarded with a rest of several minutes. If its fear prevents accomplishing this, I dismount and walk to the spot holding on to the colt with my very long lead rope. I then patiently ask the reassured colt to come toward me, a step or two at a time, never using force and waiting for habituation to occur each time I detect a desire for flight on its part.

If all of this takes twenty or thirty minutes, I consider it time well spent as a training lesson. The colt learns to trust my judgment, it is reassured rather than frightened and I have made progress in preventing future shying.

I now lead the colt back and forth, past the feared spot several times, finally stopping for a minute's rest at the spot. Then I mount and ride past the spot, back and forth, again and again, until the colt looks bored. I then stop at the spot and we rest again. The menacing place has now become a pleasant sanctuary for rest. The horse desires that spot. Repeated each time a young horse shys, the shying habit is eventually extinguished. Surely this approach makes more sense than whipping, spurring and agitating a frightened horse.

These and other problem solving techniques are shown in my video tape, *Understanding Horses*.

Food rewards can also be used to reinforce desired responses. A pinch of grain or a single pellet can serve as positive reinforcement when a horse accepts a previously feared thing.

Constantly moving the horse, whether in hand or under saddle, also serves to increase his sense of subordination to us and enhance our role as leader.

The psychology used in preventing shying can be similarly applied to any evasive behavior displayed by horses when working with them. The technique doesn't just apply to riding situations. It can be used when grooming, in farriery, for veterinary procedures and so on. As long as actual pain is not involved, horses can be desensitized to *any* frightening sensory stimulus and taught to regard it as a pleasurable thing rather than something to be feared. However, because of the horse's extraordinary memory, it is always best to use these techniques to prevent rather than to cure.

2. Pulling Back: The cause of this common misbehavior is the Opposition Reflex. The prevention is to avoid non-yielding ties using one's arms and then progressing to elastic ties. Correcting this vice is not easy once it is established. A variety of hitches have been devised to discourage pulling back by causing the horse, in effect, to "punish itself." They usually work, but horses are intelligent enough to know when such a hitch is in effect and will often revert to their previous bad habit as soon as they are tied in a conventional manner.

The most popular hitch is to place an unbreakable noose (a nylon lariat) around the girth area of the horse. Run the end of the rope through the halter and tie the horse to an elastic inner tube placed at the height of the horse's head or higher. Be sure to use a slip knot. Just in case, have a sharp knife handy. (*Always* have a sharp knife with you whenever you work around horses.) Tie the horse short and high. If he pulls back, the noose will tighten around his girth area, causing great discomfort which will only be relieved when he bounces forward. The first time such a hitch is used, it is a good idea to loop it through the inner tube, rather than tying it. Be sure the tube is on an unbreakable post or tree and that the ground is not slippery or too hard.

I remember a mare in Arizona, which was a stubborn pullback or "fly back" as we used to call them. The owner rigged a hitching post next to an irrigation canal and tied the mare with a weak, breakable lead rope. Left tied, she eventually flew back. The rope broke and she went over backwards into the canal. She never pulled back again. Remember the infallible memory of the horse.

3. Refusal to Load into a Trailer: The clinicians, who have increased in number every year since around 1980 and who are involved in what I call

"The Revolution in Horsemanship," all use technically correct behavior shaping techniques. There are minor variations in their approach, but their methods, outlined below, are essentially similar.

The horse learns a conditioned response - to move forward on command. Tapping the horse on the hindquarters with a whip, light stick or whirling the end of the lead rope does this. The instant the horse moves forward the tapping is stopped.

Once conditioned the horse is asked to move toward the trailer. Discomfort, caused by a stimulus it has been conditioned to, causes it to move forward. Whenever it moves forward the stimulus stops. The horse is rewarded with comfort. Ultimately the horse will view the trailer as a sanctuary and a refuge from discomfort.

There are many videotapes available demonstrating this version of the procedure produced by trainers teaching this kind of non-confrontational and humane horsemanship. The reader is urged to purchase such a tape and view it repeatedly before attempting to use the method. These methods work only if done correctly and accompanied by patience, tolerance and understanding.

4. Disrespect: Inevitably, at every training seminar I have conducted and at every training clinic I have attended, there are students present who complain of disrespectful behavior by their own horses. This may be as simple as ignoring the owner's presence and invasion of their personal space, or not leading obediently and quietly, to completely outrageous infractions such as kicking, biting, charging, rearing or striking. Some owners complain that they actually fear their own horses and cannot enter the stall or pen.

Respect - a subordinate attitude - in the equine species is gained by control of movement. Control the feet and you control the horse! Anytime the horse causes *you* to move he has control of you! Remember that control of movement may involve either causing movement or inhibiting it.

Many horse owners believe that when a horse comes up to them and nuzzles them (without the horse being invited to do so), this is "cute" or think, "Isn't this sweet, my horse loves me." Watch a mare control the movement of her foal. She nuzzles, nudges and pushes her foal in the direction she wants it to move. She controls the foal's movement and teaches it that she is the boss. The mare establishes respect for her position in the heirarchy. Therefore, when a horse nuzzles, nudges or pushes us, we instinctively move away (to avoid injury) and the horse has taught us to move away from it. Who's in charge? A horse should never be allowed into your "personal space" unless invited. Every time a horse comes into your space, nuzzles or nudges you, it is important to take the time to make it move back, away or off to one side. The key is consistency. It takes time and patience with consistency to establish a respectful attitude in a horse.

The SECRET to the Revolution in Horsemanship is control of movement. It is rapidly displacing the use of physical force and the infliction of pain that has characterized all disciplines of horsemanship, world wide, throughout human history.

Chapter 21

Restraint

The focus so far has been concerned with the reactions of the horse and with methods of manipulating, modifying and shaping equine behavior, using psychological means. It seems inappropriate to discuss physical methods of restraining the horse. Many of the physical means of restraint, however, have a psychological reason for their effectiveness and the subject, therefore, is pertinent to the psychology of equine behavior.

Those of us who handle large numbers of horses daily in our work, such as farriers and veterinarians, often resort to expedient measures. Even if we know that we can teach a horse to accept certain procedures using behavior-modifying techniques described earlier, we usually do not have the time to implement such techniques. Many desensitizing and counter-conditioning methods require fifteen to thirty minutes to achieve the desired effect and a busy practitioner simply does not have that much time to spare.

Also, the practitioner is not a horse trainer and should not be utilized as such by the horse-owning client. It is the client's responsibility to have the horse trained to accept farriery and routine veterinary procedures. In lieu of such training, the practitioner is completely justified to use chemical restraint. A selection of tranquilizing, hypnotic, sedative and analgesic drugs are now available to make treatment of horses easier. The important thing, in my view, is that the practitioner *not* get into a physical battle with the patient, risking injury to either horse or handlers and creating lasting distrust, fear and apprehension in the horse.

If a horse is not already trained to accept veterinary work, grooming procedures or farriery, or cannot be taught to accept them in a reasonable amount (a few minutes) of time, then the use of some form of restraint is justified. This restraint may be chemical or physical, as follows.

The Twitch: Twitching horses by applying severe pressure to some part of the body has been used since the horse was first domesticated and perhaps before then. I remember seeing a travel film in the late thirties showing a safari in East Africa. A zebra was caught with a snare held on a long pole after being chased by a truck. After the noose was around the zebra's neck several natives leaped from the truck. Two of them seized the zebra's head and bit its ears. This technique, well known to American cowboys, will usually immobilize an equine for some time, in this case until other natives were able to tie up the zebra's legs and cast it.

Common twitching devices put pressure on the animal's lip. Usually the upper lip is used, but occasionally the lower lip is also used. In a majority of cases, the application of the twitch produces several minutes of immobilization, during which frightening or even painful procedures may be performed without the animal resisting significantly.

Similarly, the tail of a foal may be flexed upward toward the backbone with sufficient pressure to immobilize the foal. Alternatively, some practitioners grasp a fold of skin where the neck joins the shoulder and twist it severely to obtain a twitch effect. This requires a strong grip and short fingernails. Horses may also be twitched by hand on the upper lip or the ear.

Pressure upon the gum under the upper lip by means of a war bridle, a chain lead shank, or a cord will also often produce an immobilizing effect. Such a device is often called a "halter-twitch" or a "bridle-twitch." I personally use this kind of device more often to sedate a horse (more about this later) or to counter-condition certain undesirable behaviors, such as head shyness, rather than using it as a twitch with steady pressure.

It is appropriate here to discuss two aspects of twitching horses. First, why does it work and how should it be done correctly?

Why does the twitch work? When I was a veterinary student, we were taught that the twitch works because of a phenomenon known as *Physiological Inhibition through Pain*. Sudden intense pain has a paralyzing effect. This is often used to immobilize an opponent in the martial arts. When a lion takes down prey, such as the Wildebeest, I

116

wonder if the lack of struggling so often seen in the unfortunate animal is due to this effect. In any case, the application of one of the twitching methods described will, in most cases, immobilize a horse, at least for a little while.

In recent years it has been popular to ascribe the immobilizing effect of the twitch to the production of endorphins by the horse's brain. Endorphins are naturally occurring opiates that are released by the body in response to stressful situations, whether they are mental or physical stresses. It is theorized that the horse stands still when twitched because it is narcotized by its own endorphins and, therefore, "feels good" and allows ordinarily painful procedures to be performed upon it. I don't buy it!

No doubt a twitched horse does release endorphins and these endorphins can be measured, but I believe that the immobilizing effect of the twitch is unrelated to these endorphins. Inhibition of movement from pain is a much more logical explanation. I believe this for several reasons.

The effect of the twitch when it works is immediate. I do not believe that endorphins can work that swiftly. If they did, then a horse suffering a sudden traumatic injury such as a fracture or a burn should immediately "feel good" and suffer no pain.

The effect of the twitch usually wears off after several minutes. *This*, I believe is the effect of endorphins. They block the pain of the twitch and therefore, the horse again becomes mobile.

Horses readily become addicted to endorphins. The addictive nature of cribbing and other stall vices (stereotypies) has recently been shown to be due to endorphin release. Indeed, some human addictions such as "runner's high" and craving for hot, peppery foods also have been traced to endorphin dependency. The subject craves the endorphins, not the 5K run or the bowl of chili. So, if twitching causes endorphin release, horses should want to be twitched. Instead most horses learn to evade and resist twitching, unless it is done cleverly and deviously, which brings us to the next concept.

How to Twitch a Horse: It is unfortunate that the twitch, an effective and defensible technique for immobilizing horses, is greatly misused and over used. When I began veterinary practice, I used the twitch all day long. I was trained to do so and it was customary to do so. Many years later, I used the twitch perhaps once a week. I had learned to control horses using a psychological approach, or with chemicals if the former approach was not practical or too time consuming. Or, I used alternative means such as flight control or pressure under the upper lip. More important, I learned to use the twitch in a more humane manner so that the patient would not resent its use.

Even head-shy horses will usually allow a finger to enter the mouth at the corner of the mouth. I do so gently and quietly and then begin to massage the upper gum, advancing gradually towards the front of the

I desensitize and sedate the horse by massaging under the upper lip. When the horse relaxes, I am able to gently insert my hand into the mouth for an examination.

Photo courtesy of Debby Miller.

mouth. If the horse becomes alarmed, I simply retreat back to where the massage was tolerated. This, of course, is simply progressive desensitization as described previously using the advance and retreat method. With rare exceptions, I am soon massaging the gum under the upper lip, above the central incisor teeth. The horse will soon act sedated, which is indicated by a lowering of the head and a sleepy expression in the eyes.

This sedating effect is ascribed to pressure at a critical acupuncture point. This may be, but I have often wondered if it is simply due to a form of oral gratification, or perhaps to the stimulation of a sense organ originating in this area of the horse's mouth, the vomeronasal organ which causes horses to "Flehman" (raise the upper lip to catch scents). The cause of the effect is academic. What matters is that it works. Horses can be sedated by pressure or massage in this area. As soon as sedation is obtained, I move my hand to the upper lip and continue to massage it. Then I slyly substitute pressure with my fingertips until the horse is "twitched," and then apply the mechanical twitch if it is needed. When treatment is completed, do not abruptly release the twitch because some horses will then react with a sudden evasive movement and many will resist twitching in the future. Instead, reverse the procedure. Replace the mechanical twitch gradually as hand pressure is applied. Then gradually substitute the severe pressure with the fingertips with gentle massage. The grateful horse has had the pain sandwiched in between two pleasant and calming experiences and in most cases, no matter how often this is done, rarely does the horse object to it. My own mules, trained to twitch in this way, can be twitched at any time and it isn't easy to fool a mule.

Many people object to "earing" a horse because they fear that the horse will become ear shy or head shy. Yet, if the above principles are observed, most horses can be repeatedly "eared" (twitched with a handhold on the ear) without causing behavior problems. There are several precautions:

- Don't twist the ear!
- Quietly and calmly massage the ear.
- *Gradually* apply fingertip pressure and with the forearm perpendicular to the ground, apply your full weight to the ear through fingertip pressure.
- When completed, *gradually* release the pressure and substitute gentle massage. Continue the massage for a minute or so, until the horse indicates relaxation and pleasure.

The previously mentioned halter twitch can also be used to sedate most horses with steady gentle pressure under the upper lip. This is not a twitch effect because the pressure required is very little. In fact, in practice, I usually placed a long brass chain shank under the lip and found that the weight of the chain alone was usually sufficient to produce a sedated expression after a minute or so.

119

Since a sharp tug on the chain will cause severe pain in such a sensitive area, the chain under the lip is a very effective means of controlling behavior in the horse. Loose, it is pleasurable and calming. Given a brief tug it is sharply painful and can be used to quickly extinguish head shyness by means of counter- conditioning. Lastly, with steady pressure, it has the same effect as a twitch - causing immobility due to the paralyzing effect of pain.

A twitch is a device that must be used with extreme caution and only if the handler is knowledgeable about the correct way to use it. It is seriously over-used and often misused. I discourage its use and encourage alternative techniques to be used whenever possible.

Hobbles: Every horse should be broke to hobbles. The horse should first be broke to one-leg hobbles in an area with soft ground and a secure, safe fence. An experienced person should do the training.

A yearling mule accepting a one-leg hobble. After accepting a one-leg hobble on each foreleg, it can be introduced to the two-leg hobble.

Photo courtesy of Debby Miller.

It only takes a few minutes to break a horse to one-leg hobbles, even when doing both front legs. The horse will always remember the lesson, even if it isn't repeated for years. Horses broke to one-leg hobbles learn to yield their legs willingly, are less likely to panic if a leg gets

120

A yearling mule readily accepts a two-leg hobble. This is a lesson
that it will not forget, even if it isn't hobbled for a long time.
Photo courtesy of Debby Miller.

caught in something and, if left hobbled and standing on three legs for ten
to fifteen minutes, develop a deeply respectful and cooperative demeanor
toward their human handlers. After the horse accepts a one-leg hobble on
each foreleg with relaxation and docility, then it can be introduced to two-
leg hobble. The first time, soft hobbles should be used.

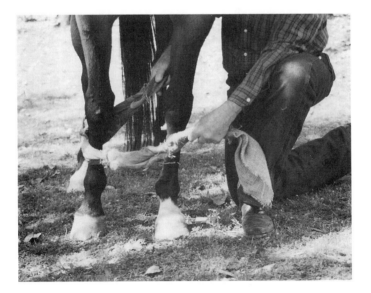

Step one: apply the hobble by placing the gunny sack around
the far leg. *Photo courtesy of Debby Miller.*

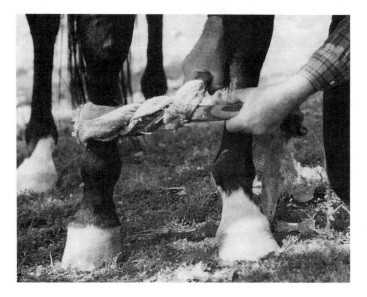

**Step two: criss-cross the ends over one another moving
toward the near leg.** *Photo courtesy of Debby Miller.*

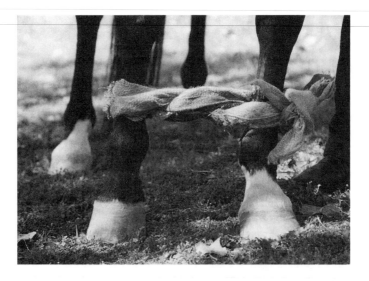

Step three: tie the ends around the opposite or near leg.
Photo courtesy of Debby Miller.

A gunny sack or braided cotton rope can be used as a hobbles and won't abrade the skin. Most horses briefly struggle when introduced to two-leg hobbles and thereafter accept hobbling without resistance. Although hobbled horses can travel surprisingly far and fast, they cannot sprint and knowing this makes them more submissive. Hobble-broke horses can be hobbled anytime in their life to stop pawing, make them stand still or to allow them to graze and still be caught afterwards.

Horses can be trained to hobble at any age. I teach the newborn foal to accept restraint of the legs and to yield the legs compliantly. When they are yearlings, I actually apply hobbles for the first time, using soft gunny sack hobbles. I teach them to accept one leg hobbles at this time.

Sensitive horse people may be horrified by the cavalier way I have discussed causing pain in horses, yet such people usually have no qualms about jerking on the bit when they ride, or riding with constant and sustained contact with the bit, both of which are painful and unnecessary riding styles.

This entire discussion emphasizes the importance of early, basic training. If horses, starting at birth, were desensitized to the frightening stimuli which accompanies veterinary procedures, farriery, grooming, transporting, training and work there would be little need for any kind of restraint later on. Moreover, if the young horse was handled in such a way that it had respect, affection and compliance toward human beings, instead of fear and distrust, much of the callousness typical of horsemanship all over the world would be eliminated.

Chapter 22

Safer Horsemanship

After you understand how the unique perceptions of the horse influence its behaviors, there are general safety rules that apply when working with horses on the ground. Anticipating a response or reaction from your horse based on his senses is paramount in knowing how to be safe. We are taught to handle all guns "as if they are loaded." Expecting horses to "blow up" at some seemingly insignificant stimulus and knowing how to stay out of the "line of fire" is the foundation of safe horsemanship. The following is a list of precautions you can take in order to be safe.

Don't work around a horse unless he is haltered or bridled. It only takes a moment to halter or bridle a horse. A horse that is free to move will do so if startled or senses some danger. The horse does not have to be tied, as long as you have hold of the lead rope or reins, you have some degree of control over its movement. Horses can be taught to "ground tie." This is an advanced skill where the horse learns to stand tied "to the ground" because the lead rope runs from the halter and appears to be "tied to the ground." The horse has actually been taught to stand still and not move at all, but it is still a good idea to have a hold of the lead rope or reins.

Announce your presence. Horses can sleep in a standing position with their eyes open. Say something quietly when you approach a horse. A startled horse will flee or may even strike or kick.

Move slowly and speak softly. Since horses are flight-oriented animals, they are easily disturbed by intense stimuli unless they have been specifically trained to ignore those stimuli. Avoid sudden, threatening gestures. A passive posture and quiet, deliberate movements are reassuring to horses. An aggressive stance, a bold approach, a fixed stare, abrupt arm or hand movements, or a harsh voice can intimidate almost any horse. Direct eye contact with a horse is intimidating. When you see a horse tense up and elevate its head, that means that it is assuming a flight position. Stop whatever you are doing and lean backwards, away from the horse. You can even drop your head and shoulders and be completely passive. Wait for the horse to relax, then slowly move toward the horse. Approach only as far as you can while the horse remains comfortable. If the horse tenses again, retreat to a passive position. Continue this advance and retreat method until you can touch the horse and stroke it. When the horse is fully relaxed you may proceed to work with the horse.

Know the safety position and try to work from that position. The safest place to stand when it is necessary to work in close contact with the horse is opposite its withers, with its head under control. There are a few procedures that can't be done from this position: taking the horse's

I examine the stifles of a young horse I have never seen before. Standing at the safety point at the shoulder, I lean toward the hindquarters, counter-balancing with my right leg. If he kicks, I am out of the way. I maintain contact which also reassures the horse.

Photo by © coco.

126

In this photo, notice that my foot is touching his left rear hoof while I examine his left stifle. *Photo by ©coco.*

temperature, looking at its teeth or trimming or cleaning its hind feet. But these procedures should at least be approached from the safety position.

Never work directly behind or directly in front of the horse. Stand off to one side if you must work with its mouth, eyes, tail or hind feet. Working in close contact next to its withers minimizes the risk of injury.

It is best if you have "three points of contact" with the horse at all times. This means that three parts of your body contact three parts of the horse's body.

For example, to clean a forefoot, while you are on the right side of the horse facing the back end of the horse, pick up the right forefoot with your left hand and bring it behind your right leg and lean into the horse with your upper arm. The horse's ankle rests on your calf and your left hand supports the foot. The three points of contact then are your upper arm, from shoulder to elbow against the horse's chest wall, the calf of your leg and your left hand. This enables you to sense relaxation, tenseness, trembling or gathering for a sudden move. Because of the horse's fast response time, no human can move fast enough to avoid a horse's kick or strike, so it is an advantage to be able to feel the horse and anticipate it's mood.

Let the horse know what you are going to do. Startling horses causes a flight reaction or a fight reaction if they cannot flee. If you are going to saddle a horse, let it first see and smell the blanket and saddle. Even a gentle, well-broke horse is deserving of such consideration. Show and let it smell the brush or curry comb before grooming. If you are going to slip a crupper under the tail or take the horse's temperature, stroke the hindquarters and progressively approach the tail. When you give a treatment by oral paste, such as medication or wormer, show the horse the tube, gently rub the horse's muzzle with the tube and then insert the tube into the corner of the horse's mouth. This method will usually permit you to handle body openings such as the nostril, mouth, eyes, or ears.

The object of safe horsemanship is to assure your horse that you will not cause it either physical or psychological discomfort and to keep yourself safe. Incorporating these techniques as habits into your horse handling methods will create a safer environment for you and your horse.

Taking the horse's temperature: I stand at the shoulder, lean forward counter-balancing by extending my left leg while sliding my hand down toward the hind end. Note the three points of contact - my left foot, my entire left side and my right hand. Reassured that the horse will tolerate my handling, I insert the thermometer. The three points of contact change to my left hip, shoulder and arm and my right hand.

Photo courtesy of Debby Miller.

129

Safer Horsemanship
Rules to Remember

- Always halter or bridle a horse before you work around or with it and have control of the lead rope or reins.
- Announce your presence when approaching a horse, it may be asleep with its eyes open.
- Avoid sudden, threatening gestures or direct eye contact with a horse.
- Always work from the safety position and maintain "three points of contact" with the horse.
- Let the horse know what you are going to do. Show the horse whatever object you are going to use: saddle, blanket, oral paste tube, grooming tools, etc.
- Wear appropriate footgear: boots with a heel high enough to keep your foot from slipping through the stirrup.
- Wear a hard hat or helmet.
- Know how to laterally control the head and neck of the horse and be able to disengage the horse's hindquarters.
- Mount and dismount at the safety position: alongside the withers.
- Know what to do when your horse "spooks."

Horses love to run, jump and play at liberty. This Thoroughbred
stallion, Gate Dancer, is shown leaping for joy and was not startled
by its handler!

Photo by Serita C. Hult.

Conclusion

Riding today in our society has become primarily a recreational activity. Horses are still vital in the ranching industry and still used for police and patrol purposes, but the majority of the horses in countries like the United States and Canada, are kept for recreational purposes. Recreation includes the sports of rodeo, racing, pleasure riding and showing horses in many different disciplines with many different breeds.

The benefits to human health, both mental and physical, from riding are not fully understood. Therapeutic riding programs for people who are physically or mentally challenged thrive because of the benefits they offer participants. The companionship and bonding that is possible between humans and horses are another benefit that transcend the physical benefit of riding. Horses kept for driving purposes, or just kept as pets can also be a source of great pleasure to their human stewards. So, for all of these reasons it is not surprising that even in our modern, industrialized, high-tech society, horses are valued, loved and increasing in numbers.

The most famous of all the nineteenth century American "horse tamers" was John Rarey. His observations are and always will be pertinent to horsemen:

> First, that the horse is so constituted by nature that he will not offer resistance to any demand made of him which he fully comprehends, if made in a way consistent with the laws of his nature.

> Secondly, that he has no consciousness of his strength beyond his experience and can be handled according to our will without force.

> Thirdly, that we can, in compliance with the laws of his nature, by which he examines all things new to him, take any object, however

frightful, around, over, or on him, that does not inflict pain, without causing him to fear.

It will at once be gathered from this that as God intended the horse for the friend, companion and servant of man, he made no blunder in so constituting the animal that men of average sense should be able to turn him to account without great trouble or any cruelty whatever.

Rarey's most famous accomplishment was his ability to tame any horse, no matter how vicious and to do it quickly. His fame spread to Europe and he did command performances for Queen Victoria.

In St. Petersburg, Russia, there is a collection of Greco-Scythic art. Included is a silver vase and on it in bas-relief, a young Scythian man lassoes a horse. Then he ties up a foreleg, puts the horse on its knees and finally has it saddled and bridled. This vase is 2,600 years old.

In DeWitt's *Complete American Farrier and Horse Doctor*, published in 1870 by Robert M. DeWitt and authored by Col. Christofer Forrest, the following profound observation appears:

> The writer of this book has no fear of being contradicted by any respectable trainer in laying it down as a fundamental principle that, other things being equal, that horse will be the best "broken," freest from trick and vice, most reliable and obedient and at the same time, the most spirited and enduring, whose course of education has been such that he cannot recall any time when he was not broken. He should have no memory of any hour of great trouble and fear when he first discovered that man was his master and, that all his struggles for freedom were in vain.

What I call "The Revolution in Horsemanship" involves training techniques which have been called "New Age Horsemanship," "Renaissance Horsemanship," "Universal Horsemanship," and especially, "Natural Horsemanship." As I predicted in 1990, this revolution will sweep the world to the benefit of the horse and all who choose to work with this unique animal.

Bibliography

Control of the Horse by Dr. Robert Miller (Lakeville, Indiana: Video Horse World, 1992). VHS Video

Early Learning by Dr. Robert Miller (Video Velocity, Virginia City, Nevada, 1995). VHS Video

Imprint Training of the Newborn Foal (Miller, R., Colorado Springs, Colorado: Western Horseman, Inc., 1991).

Influencing the Horse's Mind by Dr. Robert Miller (B & B Equestrian Video, 1984. Distributed by Miller's, Rutherford, New Jersey). VHS Video

Join up by Monty Roberts (Solvang, California: Flag is Up Farms, Inc., 1996). VHS Video

The Jeffery Method by Maurice Wright (The Farnam Company, Phoenix, Arizona, 1987) VHS Video

The Jeffery Method of Horse Handling (Wright, M., Prospect, Australia: R.M. Williams Pty., Ltd., 1973.)

Safer Horsemanship by Dr. Robert Miller (Virginia City, Nevada: Video Velocity, 1999). VHS Video

Understanding Horses by Dr. Robert Miller (Virginia City, Nevada: Video Velocity, 1998). VHS Video

Index